DAILY DISCOVERY

ELEUTHERA
PUBLICATIONS

Eleuthera Publications
Washington, D.C.

DAILY DISCOVERY
A DEVOTIONAL

David F. Allen, MD, MPH

To purchase additional copies of this book online go to:

www.dailydiscovery.info

Requests for information should be addressed to:

Eleuthera Publications
455 Massachusetts Ave. NW #150-144
Washington, DC 20020

publisher@eleutherabooks.com
www.eleutherabooks.com

ABOUT THE AUTHOR

Dr. David Allen was trained in medicine at St. Andrews University Medical School in Scotland and in Psychiatry and Public Health at Harvard Medical School where he was a Kennedy Fellow. He did work in religion, psychiatry, and ethics under Professor Arthur Dyck at the Harvard Divinity School. He has also taught psychiatry and religion at Harvard, Yale, and Georgetown Medical School.

Dr. Allen was mentored in theology by Dr. Francis Schaeffer at L'Abri Fellowship in Switzerland. He studied contemplative psychology under Dr. Gerald May at Shalem Institute in Bethesda, M.D. and psychiatry and spirituality under Fr. Henri Nouwen at Yale Divinity School.

Dr. Allen was awarded the RB Bennett Commonwealth Prize by the Royal Society of Arts in London for his international contribution in the field of cocaine addiction and treatment. He was featured in the PBS special "The Drug Wars" which documented his identification of the crack cocaine epidemic in 1985. He was one of the authors of a groundbreaking scientific article in *The Lancet*, June 1986, which heralded the crack cocaine epidemic.

Voted one of the most outstanding psychiatrists for 2002-03, Dr. Allen was also named a Distinguished Life Fellow of the American Psychiatric Association in 2008. He was honored for his work in addiction by the Royal Society of Arts in London.

He has established drug and alcohol treatment clinics in Washington, D.C. and Nassau, Bahamas. He is a popular conference speaker and has an international private practice in the Bahamas. His television show, "People Helping People," and his radio show, "Coming Home to Face Our Heart," are on the air weekly in the Bahamas.

Dr. Allen is the author of a number of books including: *Crack the Broken Promise, In Search of the Heart, Shattering the Gods Within,* and *Contemplation: Intimacy in a Distant World, Pudgy: A Bahamian Parable* and an award-winning DVD version of *Pudgy*, and *Shame: The Human Nemesis*.

A renowned psychiatrist and author, Dr. Allen is also a popular and powerful conference speaker. He has conducted conferences and seminars for many organizations including the Young Presidents Organization of Washington D.C., the Chautauqua Institute, Chautauqua, New York, and the Institute for Applied

Theology and Behavioral Sciences at the Psychiatric Institute of Washington. His widely acclaimed marriage, grief, and shame seminars have been hosted by churches as diverse as Dallas Bible Church, Dallas, Texas and St. Teresa of Avila Catholic Church, Washington, D.C.

Dr. Allen is the director of the Renascence Institute, Nassau, Bahamas where his team of psychoanalysts and therapists serve an international clientele and specialize in marital therapy, depression, grief and loss, addictions, and crisis management.

David lives in his native Bahamas with his wife, Victoria, who is an author and Associate Professor at the College of the Bahamas. Their home on the Bahamian sea is full of love and the Real Presence of Christ. Most of all, they enjoy living near their children and grandchildren.

Contact Information:

Dr. David F. Allen

The Renascence Institute
P.O. Box SP 63124 Sandyport, Nassau
The Bahamas

dfallen43@gmail.co

(301) 969-358-2192 or (242) 327-8719

ACKNOWLEDGEMENTS

I would like to express my deepest appreciation to Curt Ashburn, my publisher, editor, and colleague who helped me put this devotional together. Special thanks also to Ms. Keva Bethell, MPH who helped with the copy editing. Last but not least, my special appreciation for my dear wife, Dr. Victoria S. Allen, who is my partner and confidante. She has stood at my side throughout both good and difficult times and is the source of my inspiration to write my spiritual journal.

INTRODUCTION

The real voyage of discovery consists not in seeking new landscapes but in having new eyes.

— Marcel Proust

Life is a challenging journey from the victimhood of our false self, based in fear and shame, to the discovery of our true self, based in love and gratitude.

— David Allen

Modern life with its urgent time pressures and burgeoning technologies leaves us disillusioned and disconnected from ourselves, each other and nature. As a result, we tend to create a world where friends walk as strangers and strangers as friends. Paraphrasing Georgia O'Keeffe:

> *No one sees a flower*
> *No one makes a friend.*
> *To see a flower*
> *Takes time.*
> *To make a friend*
> *Takes time.*
> *And . . .we have no time.*

It is easy to blame our predicament on external circumstances and forget the words of the wisdom writer: "Guard your heart for out of it comes the issues of your life" (Prov. 4:23). Sadly, the heart, like a sponge, absorbs the hurt and shame of our lives. Unless we release the pain, there is no space in our heart for love.

Facing shame, which I define as **S**elf **H**atred **A**imed at **ME**, is not easy because shame buries our authentic self, encouraging us to live our lives out of an illusory false self. As we age, this false self becomes more entrenched making us puppets of our external reality and circumstances. As a result, we follow the shadow rather than the substance of our existence.

Our greatest challenge and hope is to face our hurt and shame and open our hearts to the eternal "love which never lets us go and the face which never turns away." Only in silence and stillness will we discover the vision of our authentic self filled with love, gratitude and forgiveness. As the Psalmist wrote, "Be still and know that I am God" (Ps 46:10).

In this devotional, using excerpts from my books *In Search of the Heart, Shattering the Gods Within, Contemplation: Intimacy in a Distant World* and *Shame: The Human Nemesis,* I invite you to come each day, read, and be still. If you are hurting badly inside, it will be difficult, but I challenge you to write your own reflections on what it means to discover your authentic self. As you reread the devotional each year, adding to your reflections, you will develop a deeper awareness of your soul, your true self. As you embrace your inner life, you will become a missionary to your own heart. In the words of St. Paul:

I pray that the eyes of your heart may be opened so that you may know the hope of your calling, the riches of his glorious inheritance, and the power of God's love dwelling in you.

Eph. 1:17

David F. Allen
Nassau
The Bahamas
2013

JANUARY

And we are put on this earth a little space where we might learn to bear the beams of love.

— William Blake

JANUARY 1

When he saw the crowds, he had compassion for them, because they were harassed and helpless, like sheep without a shepherd.

Matthew 9:36

BE CREATIVE

When I was a third-year psychiatric resident at Harvard in 1972, I spent part of that time in a drug treatment clinic in East Boston. It had always puzzled me that people could destroy their lives by putting chemicals into their bodies.

One client particularly frustrated me. John, a thirty-five-year-old man, had begun using marijuana and alcohol at the age of thirteen; then he went on to heroin. His family was poor; his father was an alcoholic who had abused John and his mother. We worked very intensely with John in individual and group psychotherapy and with his family in family therapy. Yet nothing changed John's behavior.

John made me realize I didn't know how to apply the traditional models of therapy to people who had given up on life and lived on the streets. Having been raised in a Judeo-Christian tradition, I struggled to integrate psychiatry and my Christian faith. This struggle was extremely difficult and caused me much emotional and intellectual turmoil.

REFLECTIONS

_____

_____

_____

_____

_____

_____

When you change the way you look at things, the things you look at change!

— Mai Mona Mohammed

*Then Cain went away from the **presence of the Lord**, and settled in the land of Nod, east of Eden.*

Genesis 4:15-17

THE TIME BOMB

John made me feel inadequate. I did not like him and I also hated myself for being so involved with him. As usual he was late for his appointment. Again I had been set up. Finally, I looked down the quiet residential street and saw John coming toward me. His blond, uncombed hair stuck straight up and out around his haggard, dirt-stained face, a rough beard showed around his chin line. He staggered left and right as he walked. Obviously, he had been drinking or shooting up.

I was almost revolted at seeing him. John must have sensed my frustration. He slurred and said words I will never forget as long as I live: "Youuuu knowwww, Dr. Allennnn, you and I are alike. Youuu see…I shoot up on heroin…and youuuu shoot up on ego." That velvet harpoon hit me in my heart. It made me realize for the first time that, yes, in many ways John and I were alike. John was dampening his pain with heroin. Was I soothing mine with ego?

John had a huge bomb inside of him, ready to explode and destroy him and anyone close to him. Yet I also had a similar explosive inside me that might go off and harm me or my family. I suspect you do too.

REFLECTIONS

_____

_____

_____

_____

A problem occurring at one level of consciousness cannot be solved at the same level.

— Albert Einstein

Then the men were even more afraid, and said to him, "What is this that you have done!" The men knew that he was fleeing from the presence of the Lord, because he had told them so.

Jonah 1:9-11

THE PRESENCE OF THE LORD

The presence of the LORD is not a geographical location. We know that God is everywhere. So the presence of the LORD is where you and I are supposed to be according to God's will. God was on that ship with Jonah just like he is with us when we disobey him. But until Jonah was in Nineveh delivering God's message, he was not in the presence of the LORD. And until we are where God has called us to be, neither will we be truly in God's presence.

REFLECTIONS

_____

_____

_____

_____

_____

_____

We shall not cease from exploration and the end of all our exploring will be to arrive where we started and know the place for the first time.

— T. S. Eliot

You hypocrite, first take the plank out of your own eye, and then you will see clearly to remove the speck from your brother's eye.

Matthew 7:5

STOP RUNNING

Have you ever felt that God was not present in your life? There is an old saying, "If you do not feel close to God, guess who moved." Jesus promised his disciples that he would never leave nor forsake them. When I contemplated leaving psychiatry a professor challenged those thoughts. "You're just running from psychiatry, Allen. Instead," he asked, "why not try to be creative within your field of psychiatry?" That professor spoke to me on God's behalf, "Don't run, David, be creative where you are." Jonah needed to be in Nineveh to be in the presence of the LORD; for me, it was not a city, but the field of psychiatry where God said he would meet me. Where is it for you?

REFLECTIONS

In the name of God, stop a moment, cease your work, look around you.

— Leo Tolstoy

They promise them freedom, but they themselves are slaves of corruption; for whatever overcomes a man, to that he is enslaved.

2 Peter 2:19

WHAT ARE YOU USING TO EASE YOUR PAIN?

As human beings, we all have hurts; we all have a sense of inadequacy, and we do different things to counteract those feelings. John shot up on heroin, I was taking large doses of ego, and others dull the pain with food, academic degrees, political or financial power. I realized the pride in my heart was alienating me from my humanness and my natural empathy with John.

In a very real sense, my own heart was hurting. How could I, who had not dealt with my own wounded heart, touch the hurting heart of John? I had to face my own pain in order to understand this. What is it that you must face before the bomb in you goes off...again?

REFLECTIONS

You don't think your way into a new kind of living. You live your way into a new kind of thinking.

— Henri Nouwen

January 6

Give ear to my words, O LORD; give heed to my groaning.

Psalm 5:1

Heart to Heart

John's words, "I shoot up on heroin, you shoot up on ego," had pierced my heart (see January 4). What John needed was a feeling response from my soul to his, not just an academic, clinical response from therapist to client. John was in touch with my heart, but I was not in touch with either his heart or my own. He was able to help me, but not himself and I, with all my training, was unable to help anyone. I had come to realize the need for empathic, heart-to-heart connection, not more psychological fads or sophisticated behavioral theories.

What could I say to a retarded child who said to me, "Fix me"?

What could I say to a mentally ill person who asked, "Why do I have to suffer so much?" Or to the twelve-year-old daughter whose mother was raped in front of her and who later asked me, "Dr. Allen, will the man come back and kill me and my family?"

Reflections

_____

_____

_____

_____

_____

_____

To be religious means passionately asking the question of the meaning of our existence and being willing to receive answers even if the answers hurt.

— Paul Tillich

The Word of God is living and active, sharper than any two-edged sword, piercing to the division of soul and spirit, of joints and marrow, and discerning the thoughts and intentions of the heart.

Hebrews 4:11, 12

THE SEARCH FOR THE HEART

The emotional pain of my clients confounded the remedies of my classical training in psychiatry. As a result of their questions and John's velvet harpoon, I was catapulted into a search for deeper meaning in my life and a search to find spontaneous, unconscious sympathy with others. This journey led me to face my pain, my inadequacy, my inner helplessness. I call this journey *the search for the heart.*

REFLECTIONS

_____

_____

_____

_____

_____

_____

Because God has made us for Himself, our hearts are restless until they rest in Him.

— St. Augustine

JANUARY 8

The light of the eyes rejoices the heart, and good news refreshes the body.

Proverbs 15:30

THE MEANING OF THE HEART

The heart is a metaphor for the center of the person, the inner core where all aspects of the person converge—the physical, the emotional, the intellectual, and the spiritual. The heart is the essence of who we really are, body, soul and spirit. I can make decisions intellectually, but **when I think through my heart,** I relate my thinking to what is happening in all aspects of my life. In the same way, when we see with our eyes, yes, we see, but when we see with our hearts, we go beyond what the eyes see to real understanding.

The heart is the place that is most personal, but also most universal since with the heart, we reach out to others. It is the dwelling place of our values, our love, our commitment, and our dreams. It is the source of our attitudes, intentions, and behavior. It is the repository of good and evil, love and hate—the place where we touch the divine.

REFLECTIONS

_____

_____

_____

_____

_____

_____

The heart has its reasons which reason knows nothing of.
— Blaise Pascal

*He drew me up from the **desolate** pit, out of the miry bog, and set my feet upon a rock, making my steps secure.*

Psalm 40:1-3

A DESOLATE HEART

When we find ourselves in a desolate pit of despair, it seems that nothing we do brings relief. We scratch and claw to climb out of the pit, but we become exhausted in body, mind, and spirit. Then we can begin to doubt that God loves us, which just leads us to more despair.

Each of us only has so much psychological energy. If we spend that energy dealing with those buried feelings, we have little or no energy left to express or feel love. Even if beauty is there, we can't see it. Even if we are loved, we can't feel it. When the heart cries out and does not receive what it needs, it finally closes, or becomes detached.

REFLECTIONS

_____

_____

_____

_____

_____

_____

Doubt is the brother of shame.
— Erik Erikson

Beloved, let us love one another; for love is of God, and he who loves is born of God and knows God. He who does not love does not know God; for God is love.

1 John 4:7-8

A MISSIONARY TO YOUR OWN HEART

Our challenge is to become missionaries to our own hearts. So often we forget the painful feelings buried deep inside us—anger, fear, shame, guilt—and the experiences that led us to feel that way. The heart is a storehouse for those painful feelings, but like a sponge it can only absorb so much emotion. Once it is saturated with pain, there's little room left for love and joy and beauty.

Often in therapy patients will say, "No one loves me." But that is not true. The truth is that their hearts are so full of hurt that they cannot feel the love around them. When hurting people have the courage to work though their pain and release the negative feelings imprisoning their hearts, it is like squeezing some of the water out of the sponge. This leaves more space in their hearts for love and joy and beauty.

REFLECTIONS

_____

_____

_____

_____

_____

_____

Amor vincit omnia, et nos cedamus amori.
Love conquers all things, so we too shall yield to love.

— Virgil

JANUARY 11

And he took the blind man by the hand, and led him out of the village; and when he had spit on his eyes and laid his hands upon him, he asked him, "Do you see anything?" And he looked up and said, "I see men; but they look like trees, walking."

Mark 8:23-24

RECOVERY AS THE PROCESS OF HEALING

Jesus' first touch of the blind man gave him enough sight to see "men like trees walking". He was no longer blind, but neither had he fully recovered his sight. True recovery means regaining what you lost during an illness or event and returning to the condition you were in before the pain began. It involves the decision to reveal the secret of your pain and share it with another, usually a therapist. Millions of people seek counseling and support every year for any number of addictions and problems. As a result, they feel better about themselves and receive inner strength to give up the destructive behavior. Recovery helps us function in everyday life.

REFLECTIONS

_____

_____

_____

_____

_____

_____

Everything can be taken from a man but one thing; the last of the human freedoms—to choose one's attitude in any given set of circumstances, to choose one's own way.

— Viktor Frankl

Then again he laid his hands upon his eyes; and he looked intently and was restored, and saw everything clearly.

Mark 8:25

FIRST, STOP THE BLEEDING

When an injured person is brought into a hospital emergency room, the doctor must first stop the bleeding. Then, after the patient is stabilized, the physician can do a more extensive examination. Life has been saved, but often there is much damage that remains. In the same way, a person with serious emotional wounds must be treated to stop the bleeding of a wounded heart. Then, after restoring physical, chemical, and emotional balance, work can begin on the process of recovery.

REFLECTIONS

_____

_____

_____

_____

_____

_____

If we hope to live not just from moment to moment, but in true consciousness of our existence, then our greatest need and most difficult achievement is to find meaning in our lives.

— Bruno Bettelheim

Like a slave who longs for the shadow,
and like laborers who look for their wages,
so I am allotted months of emptiness,
and nights of misery are apportioned to me.
When I lie down I say, 'When shall I rise?'
But the night is long,
and I am full of tossing until dawn.

Job 7:2-4

EMPTINESS

A client named Anita told me, "I am the emptiest recovering person there is." Recovery therapy is necessary, but it is not enough. Like Anita, it allows us to "see men like trees walking", but the goal is to see clearly. Just as physical therapy helps us walk after a broken bone is reset, there is another step beyond recovery therapy that helps us run again. It is like the second touch of Jesus that allowed the blind man to see "everything clearly."

REFLECTIONS

_____

_____

_____

_____

_____

_____

One sometimes weeps over one's illusions with as much bitterness as over a death.

—Guy de Maupassant

And all the people of Israel murmured against Moses and Aaron; the whole congregation said to them, "Would that we had died in the land of Egypt! Or would that we had died in this wilderness! Why does the LORD bring us into this land, to fall by the sword? Our wives and our little ones will become a prey; would it not be better for us to go back to Egypt?"

Numbers 14:1-4

BACK TO EGYPT

A recovering alcoholic confessed to me, "I have given up alcohol and drugs but now I feel empty and meaningless. At least when I used to drink I would go with the boys and have a good time. I can't take it, Doc. You have helped me give up alcohol and drugs, but I feel miserable. I am going back to my old life."

I have been saddened by this pattern many times. A distinguished and wealthy man who moved in and out of drugs, alcohol, and depression told me, "I have been through recovery over and over again. I know the Twelve Steps backward and forward. But I end up feeling empty. Something is missing."

REFLECTIONS

_____

_____

_____

_____

_____

_____

Getting over a painful experience is much like crossing monkey bars. You have to let go at some point in order to move forward.

— C. S. Lewis

JANUARY 15

Then the LORD said, "I have seen the affliction of my people who are in Egypt, and have heard their cry because of their taskmasters; I know their sufferings, and I have come down to deliver them out of the hand of the Egyptians, and to bring them up out of that land to a good and broad land, a land flowing with milk and honey....

Exodus 3:7, 8

THE WILDERNESS OF RECOVERY

In 1982, as Chairman of the National Drug Council of the Bahamas, I worked intimately with hundreds of patients addicted to crack cocaine. Tough, violent, and fragmented, they had been blown away by that terrible and powerful drug. Many of them reached a state of recovery, staying off drugs for as long as 18 months.

However, even in recovery they had severe cravings and felt isolated. They described a feeling of emptiness, and internal void. But without exception, at least in my program, any person who managed to get through this stage and remain drug free for two years were the ones who went beyond recovery to discovery.

REFLECTIONS

_____

_____

_____

_____

_____

_____

Remembering you are going to die is the best way I know to avoid the trap of thinking you have something to lose. You are already naked. There is no reason not to follow your heart.

— Steve Jobs

JANUARY 16

The LORD is near to the brokenhearted, and saves the crushed in spirit.

Psalm 34:18

WOUNDED AND BROKEN

Unfortunately, most therapy stops after recovery and the world is filled with half-blind people who can only "see men as trees walking." Therapy allows us to pick up the broken pieces of our lives and break the chains of addiction or destructive patterns that destroy relationships. However, if the process of healing stops there, you may be left with a feeling of emptiness; you may be caught up in loneliness, perfectionism, frustration, and isolation.

REFLECTIONS

_____

Someone was hurt before you, wronged before you, hungry before you, frightened before you, beaten before you, humiliated before you, raped before you... yet, someone survived... You can do anything you choose to do.

— Maya Angelou

*Pharaoh will say of the Israelites, "They are wandering aimlessly in the land; the **wilderness** has closed in on them."*

Exodus 14:3

WANDERING IN THE WILDERNESS

The goal is not just recovery. Deliverance from the slavery of Egypt is the first step, but for many people recovery is an empty wilderness where going back is a constant temptation. What is needed is discovery, leaving the wilderness and entering the Promised Land where the emptiness of recovery is filled with the "milk and honey" of a clean life.

My patients often say to each other, "I am in discovery. Are you?" They are saying that they are in a different stage from when they first recovered from their problems and addictions. In fact, discovery is available to anyone who is searching for a deeper meaning in life—**searching for his or her heart.** It is our true self, our heart that we are trying to discover.

REFLECTIONS

_____

_____

_____

_____

_____

_____

Not all those who wander are lost.

— J.R.R. Tolkien

But when he heard it, he said, "Those who are well have no need of a physician, but those who are sick...'I desire mercy, and not sacrifice.' For I came not to call the righteous, but sinners."

Matthew 9:12-13

THE BIG BREAK UP

The word *discovery* comes from the Latin prefix *dis*, which means "to break apart," and the Latin word *cooperire*, which means "to cover, to conceal." This discovery is breaking apart the false covering so the real self—the heart—though hurt and wounded, can rest complete in God's love. There is a space for God in all of us. Some call this the search for fulfillment, the desire for love, or the longing for inner peace.

REFLECTIONS

_____

_____

_____

_____

_____

_____

There is a God shaped vacuum in the heart of every man which cannot be filled by any created thing, but only by God, the Creator, made known through Jesus.

— Blaise Pascal

*Then the eyes of both were opened, and they knew that they were naked; and they sewed **fig leaves** together and made loincloths for themselves.*

Genesis 3:7

THE BIG COVER UP

Man's first response to sin or its consequences is to cover it up. As soon as Adam and Eve disobeyed God and ate from the forbidden tree, they covered themselves with fig leaves to hide their nakedness, their shame. False coverings hide our true self, the heart, and discovery is the process of removing those false coverings which we have made from the leaves of the very sins which wounded our hearts in the first place. Just like Adam and Eve, we grab the first available covering, rather than face the naked truth.

REFLECTIONS

_____

_____

_____

_____

_____

_____

This above all: to thine own self be true,
And it must follow, as the night the day,
Thou canst not then be false to any man.
— William Shakespeare

*I do not consider that I have made it my own; but this one thing I do,
forgetting what lies behind and straining forward to what lies ahead.*

Philippians 3:13

BEYOND RECOVERY

The realization of the need for discovery comes to people differently. Sometimes they do not need recovery. Yet they long for a deeper meaning to life. Discovery involves moving beyond recovery, breaking apart the hardened shell of repressed hurt. Discovery unravels the false coverings woven around the heart for self-protection, and exposing the pearl beneath. As we face our woundedness and admit our brokenness we find something beyond personality and damaged memories. We find a living spirit with a unique identity and a great capacity to love and feel loved because we are made in the image of God.

REFLECTIONS

---

*The only way of discovering the limits of the possible is to venture a little
way past them into the impossible.*

— Arthur C. Clarke

*You shall love the Lord your God with all your heart, and with all your soul, and with all your mind, and with all your strength.' [and] 'You shall love your neighbor **as yourself**.' There is no other commandment greater than these.*

Mark 12:30

A FOUR-STAGE JOURNEY

Discovery is a four-stage journey, but the stages are not in the same order for everyone. However, we will refer to them as the first, second, third and fourth stages. The stages are:

- Awareness
- Confrontation
- Commitment
- Vocation

As we have learned, the problem with recovery is that it often leaves us in a wilderness of emptiness where we are constantly looking back to Egypt. As you begin the search for your heart, take today's scripture with you and pray that the Lord will fill you with his love.

REFLECTIONS

_____

_____

_____

_____

_____

_____

Prayer begins...with a "return to the heart" finding one's deepest center, awakening the profound depths of our being in the presence of God, who is the source of our being and of our life.

— Thomas Merton

Blessed are those who hunger and thirst for righteousness, for they shall be satisfied.

Matthew 5:6

AWARENESS

Becoming aware of the need for a deeper meaning of life or a deeper walk with God is the most important prerequisite to discovery. Awareness is a state of humility that allows us to face the truth of our hearts regardless how painful. As a hungry and thirsty person searches for food and water, so a broken heart sends a person looking for discovery. This explains why the people in recovery who admit their limitations and pain are sometimes more open to seeking a deeper meaning in life than those who deny their problems.

REFLECTIONS

_____

_____

_____

_____

_____

_____

If we cannot humbly accept ourselves, we cannot love others and cannot receive affirmation from God.

— Walter Trobisch

*For it is a credit to you if, being **aware** of God, you endure pain while suffering unjustly.*

1 Peter 2:19

THE WHERE, WHAT, AND WHY OF AWARENESS

Awareness, the first stage of discovery, is where we begin to ask searching questions such as:

- *Where is my life headed?*

- *What's the purpose behind all the efforts?*

- *Why is love worth it?*

REFLECTIONS

_____

_____

_____

_____

_____

_____

He who has a why to live for can bear almost any how.
— Friedrich Nietzsche

Then you will know the truth and the truth will set you free.

John 8:32

CONFRONTATION

When no longer enslaved by drugs, cravings, and other destructive feelings and impulses, the recovered person stands unfettered at the threshold of choice. This is where I was when I began to feel overcome by the hopelessness of my patients' problems and John threw his velvet harpoon at me. Knowing the truth and making a choice to follow it to freedom are two different things.

REFLECTIONS

_____

_____

_____

_____

_____

_____

How many legs does a dog have if you call the tail a leg? Four. Calling a tail a leg doesn't make it a leg.

— Abraham Lincoln

*Teach me your way, O Lord, that I may walk in your **truth**; give me an undivided heart to revere your name.*

Psalm 86:11

CONFRONTATION: ILLUSION AND REALITY

Consider this parable of how illusion becomes reality: A slave in ancient times was chained to a stake. He walked monotonously around the stake, longing to be free. His only escape from the pain of his condition was to dream of freedom, seeing himself roaming the distant, rolling, verdant fields. In his mind he was growing corn in that lush soil and living with a wife in his own home.

According to the legend, an angel came as the slave slept and broke the chain. When the slave awoke and saw that the chain was broken, he jumped up and headed for the distant hills. Suddenly his heart filled with fear as he thought about the dangers lurking in those unknown regions. *There may be lions out there or hostile warriors who do not like me and try to hurt me. Or I might get lost. On top of that, I have never farmed before. How would I begin?*

Terrified by the prospects of the unknown, the slave walked back down the hill, grabbed the familiar-though-broken chain, and began to walk around the stake as before. As he trudged around and around in that perpetual circle, he rationalized, *this is where I've been. I know what to expect here. Maybe it is not so bad after all.* As Sir Lynden Pindling, former Prime Minister of the Bahamas, said, "Often we break the chains off of our hands, but do not remove them from our minds".

REFLECTIONS

_____

_____

_____

_____

Better even to die free than to live slaves.
— Frederick Douglass

It is for freedom that Christ has set us free. Stand firm, then, and do not let yourselves be burdened again by a yoke of slavery.

Galatians 5:1

TRUE FREEDOM

Human beings can adapt to pain as well as joy; pain can become a companion. A slave mentality will always choose bondage, even though freedom is available. Often the bondage in our own hearts enslaves us more than external restraints. Conversely, if the heart is free and unfettered, then even when we are physically imprisoned, we are freer than our captors. In a Nazi prison camp, author Viktor Frankl found far more inner freedom than his prison guards. Even in the horror of a concentration camp, Frankl knew that true freedom was the ability to determine one's own attitude and spiritual well-being. The Nazi SS guards could not control the inner life of Frankl's soul.

REFLECTIONS

_____

_____

_____

_____

_____

_____

The average man does not want to be free. He only wants to be safe.

— H. L. Mencken

Today I invoke heaven and earth as a witness against you that I have set life and death, blessing and curse, before you. Therefore choose life so that you and your descendants may live!

Deuteronomy 30:19

CHOOSE LIFE

Recall the legend of the slave whose chain was broken by the angel (January 25). His external circumstance had changed from slavery to freedom. But inside he was still a slave. He was still chained to his old ways. The angel could free him from chains of iron, but only he had the power to choose to be free from the chains of his old life. So to, we may be helped by a therapist to break the chains of addiction or other self-destructive behavior. But we will soon return to those chains if we do not discover within us our true self, our heart.

REFLECTIONS

The Christian life is not a constant high. I have my moments of deep discouragement. I have to go to God in prayer with tears in my eyes, and say, 'O God, forgive me,' or 'Help me.'

— Billy Graham

JANUARY 28

The thief comes only to steal and kill and destroy; I came that they may have life, and have it abundantly.

John 10:10

AN OVERFLOWING LIFE

The ultimate goal of discovery is not merely to recover one's capacity for healthy choices free from destructive influences. The goal is to step across the threshold of choice, deciding to take the first steps on a journey to the fullness of life that God intended for us. God does not set us free from our addictions and destructive behavior simply to wander aimlessly in the wilderness of recovery. The stability and clear mind that comes with recovery is, for most people, temporary. From the recovery we either return to Egypt, our old ways, or move on to the Promised Land and the abundant life.

REFLECTIONS

_____

_____

_____

_____

_____

_____

When you arise in the morning think of what a privilege it is to be alive, to think, to enjoy, to love....

— Marcus Aurelius, *Meditations*

*I hereby command you: Be strong and **courageous**; do not be frightened or dismayed, for the Lord your God is with you wherever you go."*

Joshua 1:9

BE STRONG AND OF GOOD COURAGE

My emphasis on moving on to discovery is in no way intended to diminish the courage and enormous effort it takes to reach recovery. But I would be doing my clients a disservice if I congratulated them and sent them on their way knowing the potential for a profound sense of emptiness that often follows leaving our addictions and destructive behaviors behind. So, if you have come this far, why not make the commitment to begin the search for your heart?

REFLECTIONS

_____

_____

_____

_____

_____

_____

Heights by great men reached and kept were not attained by sudden flight but, while their companions slept, they were toiling upward in the night.

— Henry Wadsworth Longfellow

And I am sure of this, that he who began a good work in you will bring it to completion at the day of Jesus Christ.

Philippians 1:6

COMMITTED TO WHAT?

You have a new awareness; you have confronted the reality of the emptiness that comes with overcoming addictions and destructive behaviors. The third stage of discovery is commitment. But first, you should be asking, "Commitment to what?" Good question! Let's look at some things that you are not committing to-

You are NOT committing to copying my search for David Allen's heart. The path I am on leads to the discovery of MY heart. Your path is the one that leads to the discovery of YOUR heart. Paul wrote, "Imitate me as I imitate Christ." Like Paul, others can only help you as they show you how to imitate Christ, but imitating my search is just another form of bondage; it will only lead you back into slavery. There are principles and common obstacles to watch for that your therapist or others can help you understand, but in the end, your journey of discovery is unique to you.

REFLECTIONS

_____

_____

_____

_____

_____

_____

To be nobody but yourself in a world
which is doing its best day and night to make you like
everybody else means to fight the hardest battle
which any human being can fight and never stop
fighting.

— e. e. cummings

He heals the brokenhearted, and binds up their wounds.

Psalm 147:3

SILENT PAIN

There is a level to human pain that I call the silent level, the deep pain, and the inexpressible feelings. No matter how hard we try individually to heal this pain and no matter how good the therapist is, we still need the help of God. The surgeon may cut, the physician may prescribe, the psychiatrist may listen, but only God's love can heal.

Spiritual discovery is the process of continually yielding or surrendering to God the wounded self--the heart--for growth and development. This is a complete revolution (a "metanoia") in which we move away from our false self, our selfish heart, to be open to God's love. As growth continues, the repressed material moving from our unconscious is given over to God. The result is a renewal in the spirit--the creation of a new heart — or what I call the development of the mature self.

REFLECTIONS

_____

_____

_____

_____

_____

_____

Language ... has created the word 'loneliness' to express the pain of being alone. And it has created the word 'solitude' to express the glory of being alone.

— Paul Tillich

FEBRUARY

Life batters and shapes us in all sorts of ways before it's done... The original, shimmering self gets buried so deep that most of us hardly end up living out of it at all. Instead we live out of all the other selves which we are constantly putting on and taking off like coats and hats against the world's weather.

— Frederick Beuchner

FEBRUARY 1

Humble yourselves in the sight of the Lord and he will lift you up.

James 4:10

HUMILITY

Humility and the search for the heart are intertwined. Sometimes, although we set out to minister to others in the power of God, dependent upon His grace, we somehow ease into a Sir Lambert-style attitude when we assume that everything rests upon us, believing:

> We are God's gift to needy people.
> We have to know everything.
> We have to be everything.
> We have to be totally available.

Pride and perfectionism become our taskmasters, and self-righteousness soon follows. Then the ends we wanted to achieve somehow get twisted to become the means to our own advancement, satisfaction, and image as "good" people. Without humility, we fall away from the simplicity of trusting God to help us and others.

REFLECTIONS

_____

_____

_____

_____

_____

_____

Beware the barrenness of a busy life.

— Socrates

February 2

A double-minded man is unstable in all his ways.

James 1:8

The Simple Life

At times all of us ache to do less and have it matter more. Anxiety over responsibility can elevate our stress levels very quickly. Simplicity is a welcome antidote to the mad rush of modern living. But true simplification does not mean merely adjusting one's schedule or ordering one's environment, although those are often necessary changes for our well-being. A cluttered heart leads to a cluttered schedule; an undivided heart leads to simplicity.

Reflections

The older I grow the more clearly I perceive the dignity and winning beauty of simplicity in thought, conduct, and speech: a desire to simplify all that is complicated and to treat everything with the greatest naturalness and clarity.

— Pope John XXIII

February 3

The LORD is my light and my salvation; whom shall I fear? The LORD is the strength of my life; of whom shall I be afraid?

Psalm 27:1

The Secret of Security

During my first year of psychiatric residency at Harvard, I had the opportunity to listen to several nuns who had decided to leave their religious work to enter secular service. Perplexed, I asked to speak to the Mother Superior. I wondered how she felt about the nuns leaving the convent. The Mother Superior gently explained that she had joined the convent to accomplish her mission of serving God. She continued, "If God chooses to show me that working at the convent no longer serves my mission, His will be done. I will continue to carry out my mission in some other way. If God calls my sisters somewhere else, they should go there to serve Him."

This dear lady of God was saying her vocation came first—and that could occur in the convent or outside of it. And she extended that freedom to others. The secret of this woman's security was her deep faith in God and her commitment to worship and serve Him at any cost.

Reflections

_____

_____

_____

_____

_____

_____

To go wrong in one's own way is better than to go right in someone else's.

— Fyodor Dostoevsky

FEBRUARY 4

Humble yourselves therefore under the mighty hand of God, so that he may exalt you in due time.

1 Peter 5:6

COMMITMENT TO FOLLOW

Anita, the same client who told me during her recovery, "I am the emptiest recovering person there is," finally made a commitment to yield her wounded heart and surrender her silent pain to God. One day she came into the clinic and said, "I have a new outlook on life. I have made a decision to submit myself completely to God's love and receive His forgiveness." Anita had made a decision to become a missionary to her own heart. This is DISCOVERY!

REFLECTIONS

_____

_____

_____

_____

_____

_____

Worry does not empty tomorrow of its sorrow; it empties today of its strength.

— **Corrie Ten Boom**

FEBRUARY 5

Peter turned and saw following them the disciple whom Jesus loved....
When Peter saw him, he said to Jesus, "Lord, what about this man?"
Jesus said to him, "If it is my will that he remain until I come, what is that
to you? Follow me!"

John 21:20-22

WILLING TO SURRENDER

Yielding, submitting, surrendering to God, they all mean the same thing. In our scripture for today, Peter wanted to know what would happen to another disciple. Jesus said, "What is that to you? Follow me!" which meant, "that is none of your business, Peter. Your only concern should be what it means for YOU to follow me." That is the commitment we talked about on February 1. Remember that I told you that you cannot copy me, you can only imitate Christ? That is exactly what Jesus is saying to Peter and he is saying it to you and to me, "Follow me."

REFLECTIONS

_____

_____

_____

_____

_____

_____

Destiny is not a matter of chance; it is a matter of choice. It is not a thing
to be waited for; it is a thing to be achieved.

— William Jennings Bryan

A new commandment I give to you, that you love one another; even as I have loved you, that you also love one another. By this all men will know that you are my disciples, if you have love for one another.

John 13:34-35

The Meaning of Following Christ

We must grasp this one central truth of the Gospel: the one sign that we are followers of Jesus is love for others. We can cover ourselves with all kinds of religious fig leaves like going to church, using lots of religious language, we can make a show of our generosity and carry a big Bible, but if we do not love one another, we do not love God, period. This is the key to discovering your heart; it is a journey toward love.

I believe that Christ wants us to relate to each other as He related to His disciples during the Last Supper — with love, with communion, with commitment despite resistance, with humility, with simplicity, with willingness to serve and be served, and within a transcendent perspective. We will learn more about these seven attitudes of the heart as we continue our journey.

Reflections

_____

_____

_____

_____

_____

_____

Humility does not mean thinking less of yourself than of other people, nor does it mean having a low opinion of your own gifts. It means freedom from thinking about yourself at all.

— Archbishop William Temple

FEBRUARY 7

Come unto me, all ye that labour and are heavy laden, and I will give you rest.

Matthew 11:28

THE DANGERS OF SELF-IMPORTANCE

We doctors, perhaps more often than most individuals, can become inflated with our importance because we are often involved in literal life-or-death situations. When I was working hard at fighting the war against the drug epidemic in the Bahamas, balancing my family life, and trying to make my medical practice run smoothly, I was sometimes overwhelmed. The responsibilities were so great, and I was so limited, so exhausted.

I came home one evening, rested my head in my hands, and released it all to God. For several moments I humbly bowed in prayer and remained silent before God. As I gave everything over to God, the very heavy load of work and concerns I had been carrying slid off my back. I rested. I felt a precious freedom—as though I had suddenly been set free from the weight of the world.

REFLECTIONS

_____

_____

_____

_____

_____

_____

To be trusted is a greater compliment than being loved.
— George MacDonald

February 8

I can do all things through him who strengthens me.

Philippians 4:13

The Habit of Discouragement

Change is not easy. Compulsions and addictions tag along on our journeys of life unless we actively break away from them.

Consider the habit of discouragement. Perhaps when things went wrong in the past we gave in to feelings of helplessness, hopelessness, and unworthiness—a common threesome. Rather than follow our inner convictions to do things differently, we may bow codependently to the dictates of the circumstances or people around us. *He won't like me if I do this,* or *they will think I am stupid,* or *I may fail and people will laugh at me,* or *I can't make it, I am too weak.*

On other occasions we may resist our own progress with "if-only" arguments: *If only I had a better education,* or *If only I had a better marriage,* or *If I had a better job,* or *If I had more time,* or *If my family understood,* or *If my church were more supportive.* All these are in fact internal resistances preventing us from achieving our true potential.

Reflections

Living and loving go together and until you start loving, you will not start living.

— Dr. Samuel Hines

By this shall all men know that you are my disciples, if you have love one to another.

John 13:35

The Necessity of Communion

We were created for communion; it is a basic requirement for meaningful human relationships. In Genesis, the Book of Beginnings, it is written, "It is not good that man should be alone." As a result God gave man a helpmate for companionship and fellowship—for communion.

Communion implies that we are not alone. I mentioned earlier that it is not the pain in childhood that injured our hearts, but the sense that no one supported us through that pain. Communion—community—gives us that support. Community helps us have the courage to reflect on our painful feelings and then open our hearts to love. David's and my life were somewhat threatened by our hazardous jaunt to Rose Island, but the pain—the fear of the dangers that arose—was lightened by our communion. Community is an essential step in the path to discovery.

Reflections

_____

_____

_____

_____

_____

_____

I would rather walk with a friend in the dark, than alone in the light.

— Helen Keller

FEBRUARY 10

You will keep him in perfect peace, whose mind is stayed on you,
because he trusts in you.

Isaiah 26:3

FROM LONELINESS TO SOLITUDE

The first movement of the spiritual life according to Henri Nouwen is from loneliness, the experience of feeling totally abandoned, to solitude, being at peace with oneself. A person who is lonely, restless, and insecure seeks relief in anything to break the sense of being isolated—telephone calls, alcohol, gossip, and even destructive behavior.

Solitude requires the development of the self so one can be nourished by the memories of past meaningful experiences, rather than frantically seeking new experiences. Solitude requires reducing the noise around us to hear the true music of our hearts. It means moving beyond the pangs and craving for human contact to listen to the voice of God, or as someone has said, to hearing the music of angels.

REFLECTIONS

The spiritual journey involves three basic movements: loneliness to solitude, hostility to hospitality, and illusion to prayer. Each word represents a pole to which we are attracted. These... poles are each a continuum along which we make our spiritual journey.

— Henri Nouwen

Bear with each other and forgive one another if any of you has a grievance against someone. Forgive as the Lord forgave you.

Colossians 3:13

FROM HOSTILITY TO HOSPITALITY

The second movement of the spiritual life according to Henri Nouwen is from hostility to hospitality. From childhood, most of us have suffered multiple losses, rejections, or different types of abuse—our hurt trail. Because of the inability of our caretakers to be there for us, many of these hurts have been repressed and remain unresolved. They have turned our hearts into infernos of hostility that separates us from ourselves and each other. Yet our hearts thirst for communion.

REFLECTIONS

_____

_____

_____

_____

_____

_____

When we want to be really hospitable, we not only have to receive strangers but also to confront them by an unambiguous presence, not hiding ourselves behind neutrality but showing our ideas, opinions and life style clearly and distinctly.

— Henri Nouwen

February 12

In your anger, do not sin. Do not let the sun go down while you are still angry, and do not give the devil a foothold.

Ephesians 4:26-27

Anger over Hidden Hurts

Helen was distant and disinterested toward others. She described growing up in a cold home with an abusive father and a very detached mother. She spent most of her time hidden away in her room, burying her hurt and anger in secret, and feeling sorry for herself. Though Helen was brilliant at school, her anger was diverted into academic supremacy, especially over the boys in her class. She had no friends.

Eventually Helen met a woman who shared the Judeo-Christian belief that God loved her. The woman showed Helen how this love was validated in Christ's incarnation and redemptive sacrifice. Helen underwent a deep spiritual movement from hostility to hospitality.

Reflections

_____

_____

_____

_____

_____

_____

Of the Seven Deadly Sins, anger is possibly the most fun. To lick your wounds, to smack your lips over grievances long passed, to roll over your tongue the prospect of bitter confrontation still to come, to savor to the last toothsome morsel both the pain you are given and the pain you are giving back — in many ways it is a feast fit for a king. The chief drawback is that what you are wolfing down is yourself. The skeleton at the feast is you.

— Frederick Buechner

Pray without ceasing.

1 Thessalonians 5:17

FROM ILLUSION TO PRAYER

The third movement of the spiritual life according to Henri Nouwen is from illusion to prayer. We humans have eternity stamped in our hearts. But this desire for immortality and transcendent meaning can be destroyed by the mundane; then it becomes an illusion, rather than reality. The illusion whispers, *Things will always be as they are. I can somehow stop the clock and enter eternity unaffected by age or death or the consequence of choice.* Tragedy, illness, death, or poor finances unmask the illusion and remind us of the fragile and transitory nature of life.

One of the cruelest lies associated with this illusion is the belief that we can pass up an opportunity to express love to those we care about because there is always tomorrow. Opportunities for heartfelt conversation are lost. Discovery calls us to live in truth and reality, making the most of the time we are allotted on earth.

REFLECTIONS

Sometimes people don't want to hear the truth because they don't want their illusions destroyed.

— Friedrich Nietzsche

FEBRUARY 14

I can will what is right, but I cannot do it. For I do not do the good I want, but the evil I do not want is what I do. Now if I do what I do not want, it is no longer I that do it, but sin which dwells within me.

Romans 7:17-21

THE DYNAMICS OF PAIN

When we begin to understand the dynamics of our pain and who has hurt us, it is easy to turn on those responsible and seek vengeance. A lack of compassion towards those who have hurt us can generate enormous anger and resentment. True healing means being willing to say to the parent, husband, wife, child, or friend who hurt you, "I forgive you and I still love you." Sometimes, due to self-loathing, we need to say this even to ourselves.

REFLECTIONS

_____

_____

_____

_____

_____

The descent into Hell is easy.
— **Virgil,** *Aeneid*

FEBRUARY 15

The Lord is good to all, and his compassion is over all that he has made.

Psalm 145:9

THE POWER OF COMPASSION

Compassion is the death blow to our Ego Addictive False Self and shame core. Are we compassionate towards our families, ourselves, our neighbors, and the world? Compassion expands our capacity for intimacy even in little things. How do we respond when someone makes a mistake that causes us a minor headache? Do we feel anger and self-righteous indignation or do we see ourselves in the faults of others and offer the same compassion we would desire to have others show us? Perhaps we feel both anger and compassion and can learn to act only on the compassion.

REFLECTIONS

_____

_____

_____

_____

_____

_____

Our task must be to free ourselves by widening our circle of compassion to embrace all living creatures and the whole of nature and its beauty.

— Albert Einstein

FEBRUARY 16

Let us not become conceited, competing against one another, envying one another.

Galatians 5:26

GUARDING AGAINST ENVY

Grudges result from the hardness of our heart. After David killed Goliath, the women shouted, "King Saul has killed his thousands, but David has killed his tens of thousands." A jealous and angry King Saul nursed his hurt allowing his anger to organize in his heart. As a result, an evil spirit – negative energy – entered King Saul. There it festered and he developed a very severe and murderous grudge against David. Saul spent the rest of his life trying to kill David (I Sam. 18:6-72).

REFLECTIONS

_____

_____

_____

_____

_____

_____

O, beware, my lord, of jealousy;
It is the green-ey'd monster, which doth mock
The meat it feeds on.

— William Shakespeare

February 17

Be angry but do not sin; do not let the sun go down on your anger....
Ephesians 4:26

The Honesty of an Authentic Faith

The often painful journey toward authentic faith requires a total commitment to brutal honesty in how we deal with our anger. We must learn to face all our unprocessed hurts and resentments. By the grace of God, we have to break up the unplowed ground of our hearts which harbors all of these deep hurts and resentments, some of which took place years ago.

Reflections

_____

_____

_____

_____

_____

_____

I know well what I am fleeing from but not what I am in search of.
— Michel de Montaigne

FEBRUARY 18

O LORD...give me an undivided heart, that I may fear your name.

Psalm 86:11

THE FRAGMENTED HEART

Our hearts and minds are constantly fragmented between work, home, family, friends, and our own selves. My mother would come home from work and say, "Let me catch myself." I always wondered what she meant. Now, as an adult, I understand that the pressures of the day spread our hearts thin over many activities and concerns. My mother needed that moment after work to compose herself in order to truly open up to her family in love. Just a brief moment of contemplation and stillness defragments and calms the heart and mind.

REFLECTIONS

We prefer to be ruined, rather than changed!

— W. H. Auden

When he saw the crowds, he had compassion for them, because they were harassed and helpless, like sheep without a shepherd.

Matthew 9:36

CREATED TO WORSHIP

Human beings are made in the image of God, the *imago dei* (Gen. 3:1). We all need to either worship God (authentic faith) or to convey god-like status to a person, situation, thing, or problem. The goal of human existence is to search for ultimate meaning. As a result, we worship whatever we consider to be the ultimate.

REFLECTIONS

_____

_____

_____

_____

_____

_____

Anything to which we are deeply committed can become a 'god'. Money, power, possessions, pleasure, scientific certitude and religious dogma are among the leading gods of our age. Insofar as none of these can bring us ultimate happiness or fulfillment, they are false idols. We worship them not out of love, but out of an unconscious need for power.

— Diarmuid O'Murchu, M.S.C

FEBRUARY 20

You will not surely die....Your eyes will be opened, and you will be like God.

Genesis 3:4-5

WHAT WE WORSHIP

From time immemorial there lies in the heart of human beings a desire to transcend the pathos, fear, and tragedy of life by projecting our will and passion to deify or empower different aspects of our lives, such as people, money, situations, religion, family, drugs. When we do not worship God in authentic faith, we do not worship *nothing*. Rather, being in the image of God, we create our own gods. The temptation to be God or to make pseudo gods out of that which is less than God began in the Garden of Eden when Satan offered Eve the forbidden fruit and reassured her with the words "you will be like God".

REFLECTIONS

_____

_____

_____

_____

_____

_____

A pseudo god or idol represents an object of central passion, a craving for power, possessions or fear.

— Erich Fromm

February 21

He is the radiance of God's glory and the exact representation of his being.

Hebrews 1:3

Created for Fellowship

God created us in his image for union and fellowship with him. When we fall short of God's holy standard, our deep narcissism alienates us from God, others, the cosmos, and our own self. Nevertheless, the *Hound of Heaven* sought reunion with us by sending his son who is "the radiance of God's glory and the exact representation of his being" (Heb. 1:3). Through the incarnation, Christ emptied himself and became one of us. He accommodated himself to our limitations, but without sin. This allows us to abide in him and discover that God is with us!

Reflections

_____

_____

_____

_____

_____

_____

Living and loving go together and until you start loving, you will not start living.

— Dr. Samuel Hines

February 22

Faith is the substance of things hoped for, the evidence of things not seen.

Hebrews 11:1

The Pseudo god of Materialism

The pseudo god of materialism reverses this implying that you can only believe what you see and you possess only what you can touch. Therefore, we worship the temporal and ignore the invisible. In our culture, the pseudo god of materialism is manifested by possessions, the repression of beauty, and technological innovation.

Reflections

_____

_____

_____

_____

_____

_____

Our Lord trusted no man; yet He was never suspicious, never bitter, never in despair about any man, because he put God first in trust...

— Oswald Chambers

Man does not live by bread alone,but by every word that comes from the mouth of God.

Matthew 4:4

The First Temptation of Christ

In the first temptation of Christ, the evil one challenged Jesus to turn stones into bread, to prove that he was the Son of God. Satan was saying to Christ that by providing for the physical needs of human beings, he would become a hero who would always be in demand. Our Lord in turn replies, "Human beings cannot live by bread alone, but by every word that comes from the mouth of God". Jesus was stressing to us the importance of feeding ourselves spiritually in order to experience the deeper meaning of life.

Reflections

_____

_____

_____

_____

_____

_____

He armed himself with the weapon that had wounded him.
— **Victor Hugo**, *Hunchback of Notre Dame*

FEBRUARY 24

Do not put the Lord your God to the test.

Matthew 4:7

THE SECOND TEMPTATION OF CHRIST

In the second temptation, our Lord was challenged to jump from the pinnacle of the temple – the temptation of the spectacular. The idea was that the leap would be so spectacular that people would be impressed and believe in him. Responding in authentic faith, our Lord told Satan, "It is also written: 'Do not put the Lord your God to the test'" (Matt. 4:5-7). It was a solemn warning against substituting a pseudo god for true faith.

REFLECTIONS

_____

_____

_____

_____

_____

_____

Hold high the cross so I can see it through the flames!
— **Joan of Arc**, last words as she was burned at the stake

And he said to him, "All these I will give you, if you will fall down and worship me." Jesus said to him, "Away with you, Satan! for it is written, 'Worship the Lord your God, and serve only him.'"

Matthew 4: 9, 10

THE THIRD TEMPTATION OF CHRIST

In the third temptation of Christ, the evil one took our Lord up on a high mountain and promised to give him all the kingdoms of the world if he would bow down and worship him. Our Lord counters by saying, "'Worship the Lord your God, and serve him only" (Matt. 4: 9, 10).

Out of this temptation comes the dynamics of pride and power as compensation for the humiliation schema of shame. These are the foundation of two modern idols: the *illusion of permanence* and the *bane of the extraordinary*.

REFLECTIONS

_____

_____

_____

_____

_____

_____

Idolatry...comes in forms we are not accustomed to recognize as readily. One is the idolatry of family. Whenever it becomes more important to do or say what will keep the family matriarch or patriarch happy than it is to do or say what God wants you to do or say, we have fallen prey to the idolatry of family. Family togetherness has become an idol and often a most oppressive one.

— Scott Peck

FEBRUARY 26

You do not even know what will happen tomorrow. What is your life? You are a mist that appears for a little while and then vanishes. Instead, you ought to say "If it is the Lord's will, we will live and do this or that."

James 4:14-15

WORSHIPING THE STATUS QUO

Unconsciously, we become so accustomed to the way things are that we are seduced into believing that things will always be as they always have been. This happens in regard to sickness and health, wealth and poverty, power and powerlessness. Life involves change, all change involves loss, and all loss involves pain. Nevertheless, we plan our lives with little thought and prayer for God's guidance or will. We worship the status quo with the illusion that we are the masters or victims of our fate.

Our Lord reminds us of the rich man who, after rebuilding his barns, said to himself that he would spend the rest of his life enjoying his wealth, but he was told, "Tonight your soul is required of you" (Luke 12:13-21).

REFLECTIONS

_____

_____

_____

_____

_____

_____

Much violence is based on the illusion that life is a property to be defended and not to be shared.

— Henri Nouwen

FEBRUARY 27

O, death where is your sting
O, grave where is your victory?

I Corinthians 15:55

HE TOOK OUR SHAME

Our Lord was victorious over all of Satan's temptations. He did not need the compensation of an Ego Addictive False Self as a defense against the deep pain of shame. Unlike us, our Lord did not have a hurt trail of shame and yet he was abandoned, rejected, and humiliated on the cross. He suffered shame, but whose shame did he die for if not his own? The answer is that he suffered for our shame once and for all giving us the power to walk in victory over shame.

Because Jesus our Lord lives, we can now face life with courage, hope, and patience. Most of all, we can now say in the words of the famous composer Johann Sebastian Bach, "Come thou sweet death" and with the apostle Paul "for me to live is Christ and to die is gain" (Philippians 1:21).

REFLECTIONS

_____

_____

_____

_____

_____

_____

Prayer begins not so much with "considerations" as with a "return to the heart" finding one's deepest center, awakening the profound depths of our being in the presence of God, who is the source of our being and of our life.

— Thomas Merton

Do not be deceived. God cannot be mocked. A man reaps what he sows.

Galatians 6:7

SHATTERING THE FALSE GODS

The wise men in T. S. Eliot's "The Journey of the Magi" returned to their kingdoms forever changed after seeking and worshiping the Christ child saying:

> *We returned to our places, these Kingdoms,*
> *But no longer at ease here, in the old*
> *dispensation,*
> *With an alien people clutching their gods.*
> *I should be glad of another death.*

Moses came down from the mountain to find the people worshiping the golden calf. He was revolted by this counterfeit god. He had just been in the presence of the true God, the Holy Other. He became enraged and confronted the people about their loyalties. Many died as the camp was purged of idolatry. When false gods are shattered, there is always much pain, disillusionment, and destruction:

REFLECTIONS

_____

_____

_____

_____

_____

_____

It is hard to live without hearing the angels sing.

— David F. Allen

MARCH

The real voyage of discovery consists not in seeking new landscapes, but in having new eyes.

— Marcel Proust

MARCH 1

Little children, keep yourselves from idols.

I John 5:21

THE FALSE SELF

John warns us about pseudo gods. This is not easy. Authentic faith in the true God requires vigilance, faithfulness, and loyalty. It means letting go of our Ego Addictive False Self - with its tendencies to self-absorption, self-gratification and control - to surrender to God and to rest in his abiding and unfailing love. In so doing, we experience our true identity as the *beloved of God.*

REFLECTIONS

_____

_____

_____

_____

_____

_____

Repentance begins, however, not with preoccupation with one's self, but with the contemplation of the holiness of Christ's gift.

— Alexander Schmemann

MARCH 2

If God is for us, who can be against us?

Romans 8:31

LEARNING TO LET GO

Surrender is not denial or resignation. It means letting go of our fears, negativity, and hopelessness to allow our true self – our being – to regroup and become refreshed to face our problems. Surrender brings us the awareness and resolve not to confuse *being* with circumstances. Our life situation is not our being. Our being is not and cannot be characterized. For example, I am *rich*, I am *poor*, I am *sick*, I am *well*, etc. Regardless of my life situation, *I am*, i.e. my being is intact.

Surrender is letting go of our life situation to open to the true essence of being and its connectedness to the *Eternal Being*, the unfathomable mystery. As we open to our essential being, we open to God who is all powerful and all knowing.

REFLECTIONS

_____

_____

_____

_____

_____

_____

The tragedy is that our eternal welfare depends upon our hearing and we have trained our ears not to hear.

— A. W. Tozer

MARCH 3

God said, "I AM who I AM."

Exodus 3:14

OPENING UP TO ETERNAL LOVE

The burgeoning pressures of life so deeply burden us that it is becoming increasingly more difficult to show up for our lives. One man told me, "I have a great life, but I have not been able to show up for it." We often feel alone, disconnected. We idolize our fears, problems, and life circumstances. By worshiping idols or our illusions, we lose the grace that is given to us (Jonah 2:8). Like Peter walking on the water, when we lose the awareness of that love, we lose courage, become overwhelmed, and sink. Only in surrender can we walk on the water in the midst of life's waves and wind.

It simply cannot be repeated enough: surrendering means letting go of fear and opening to the *Eternal Love* that *has always been* before, *is* now, and *will be* forever. When we surrender, our small *i* is swallowed up in the loving, protective arms of the great '*I AM*'.

REFLECTIONS

Trust is the experience of being gazed upon by the delighted other.

— Erick Erickson

MARCH 4

Behold! The Lamb of God who takes away the sin of the world!

John 1:29

SEE A FLOWER

So often in the hustle and bustle of daily experience, our life is filled with negativity, anger, fear, and resistance. Burgeoning reports of bad news often leave us frustrated and depressed. We are constantly challenged and overcome by stressful lifestyles, urgent time pressures, and ever increasing demands.

Nevertheless, peace is possible through the awareness of God's love, but this awareness is only possible in surrender. Many of us do not come to awareness without the challenge of illness, tragedy, or suffering. As one man said, "I did not learn stillness until I suffered illness." We must live in the awareness that surrender is possible. There is love in fear, peace in the storm, hope beyond despair, a "balm in Gilead".

REFLECTIONS

_____

_____

_____

_____

_____

_____

No one sees a flower
No one makes a friend
To see a flower takes time
To make a friend takes time
And we have no time.

— Georgia O'Keefe

MARCH 5

Choose you this day whom you will serve...as for me and my house, we will serve the Lord.

Joshua 24:15

CHOICE

Surrender is a choice. We can choose the tyranny of our circumstances by continuing to live in fear and negativity or we can choose to surrender to God, the source of love and the ground of our being. Choice is cataclysmic. It can make the difference between living in hell or heaven.

Victor Frankl was imprisoned in the concentration camps of Germany. In his memoirs, he said that when he discovered that he alone was responsible for his choices, he chose to live with a positive attitude. At that point, he became free and his captors were imprisoned.

We, too, can choose to surrender or be destroyed. To surrender is to choose freedom from the shackles of despair and to open up to the eternal freedom of love. Positive attitudes keep us focused and present. Negative attitudes are destructive and produce ongoing negativity, anger, fear, and despair. Positive attitudes encourage us to be proactive, to focus on solutions rather than problems.

REFLECTIONS

_____

_____

_____

_____

_____

_____

You cannot love a fellow creature fully till you love God.

— C.S. Lewis

MARCH 6

Son of man, you are living among a rebellious people. They have eyes to see but do not see and ears to hear but do not hear, for they are a rebellious people.

Ezekiel 12:2

THE PERCEPTUAL SHIFT

Essentially there are two basic feelings – love and fear. All feelings tend to encompass or are connected with one of these two. The perceptual shift moves our point of view from fear to love. The deeper our shame, the harder it is for us to make the transition from fear to love. Surrender makes the perceptual shift from fear, resistance, and negativity to the freedom of humility, peace, and compassion. The insight of this dynamic has blessed my life and many others. It is a conscious, simple, and a reliable way to practice surrender. When we surrender, we place ourselves in the love which never lets us go, and the gaze of the face which never turns away.

REFLECTIONS

_____

_____

_____

_____

_____

_____

Detachment doesn't mean you don't let the experience penetrate you. On the contrary, you let it penetrate you fully. That's how you are able to leave it.

— Mitch Albom

March 7

Give thanks to the LORD, for he is good; his love endures forever.

Psalm 107:1

Gratitude

Expressing gratitude opens us to love. Gratitude is a portal into the unmanifested. Gratitude frees us from our Ego Addictive False Self. Gratitude opens our hearts to the experience of love which is our true identity. I was shocked when a deeply hurt female cocaine addict said, "Dr. Allen, in the crack house, I have come to realize that the addict who is grateful for one day sober, soon surrenders and moves on to sobriety."

Expressing gratitude for life, family, job, etc., frees us to be who we are. Gratitude is the humble acceptance and acknowledgement of God's love for us. Surrender prevents complaining and empowers us to act positively with gratitude. Without gratitude there is no surrender and our negativity leads to despair and frustration. Even if we are successful in addressing the problem, we are left empty, unsettled, and looking for the next problem because our consciousness is identified with thought and problem solving.

Reflections

At times our own light goes out and is rekindled by a spark from another person. Each of us has cause to think with deep gratitude of those who have lighted the flame within us.

— Albert Schweitzer

MARCH 8

Humble yourselves before the Lord, and he will lift you up.

James 4:10

HUMILITY

Humility is a prerequisite for surrender. But it is also the result of surrender. Surrender is only possible if there is an intentional desire to be humble. Humility is opening up to accept who we are and not who we wish to be, acknowledging where we are and not where we wish to be. The Ego Addictive False Self with its self-absorption, high experience seeking tendencies, and pride (control and arrogance), defends against our deepest hurt or shame. It blocks us from experiencing who we are (true self), it catapults us into a defensive retinue of wishful illusion of being anything but who we actually are.

The road to humility is strewn with the stones of humiliation. Humiliation in love drives us to humility and opens us to surrender. Waves of humility usually precede surrender. Sadly, we often have to be broken. I do not say this lightly because much pain is involved.

REFLECTIONS

_____

_____

_____

_____

_____

_____

If you plan to build a tall house of virtues, you must first lay deep foundations of humililty.

— St. Augustine

Come unto me all ye that labor and are heavy laden, and I will give you rest.

Matthew 11:28

LETTING GO

Change is an external phenomenon, a situational shift, e.g., moving from house A to house B. Transition, on the other hand, is an internal phenomenon that takes place in our hearts. We may make the physical change from house A to house B, but in transition it is possible for our heart to still be at house A. In transition we have to let go of how things used to be and take hold of the way they are. In between letting go and taking hold again, there is a chaotic but potentially creative neutral zone where things are not the old or new way.

We do not usually resist change because change just happens. We resist transition because it is emotional and slow moving. Resisting transition occurs because we find it hard to let go of that part of our heart which is embedded in how things used to be. Transition takes longer than change and requires letting go of negativity, resistance, and fear.

REFLECTIONS

_____

_____

_____

_____

_____

_____

Letting go in transition involves disengagement, disidentification, disenchantment, and disorientation.

— David F. Allen

March 10

When he saw the crowds, he had compassion for them, because they were harassed and helpless, like sheep without a shepherd.

Matthew 9:36

Disengagement

Disengagement means giving up the old reality to open to the new, breaking away from former roles and activities. Psychological disengagement is particularly difficult because human beings find it hard to say goodbye. When we do say goodbye, it is fraught with sadness, anger, resistance, regret, and obstinacies. But if we cannot say goodbye, it is hard to say hello. Effective disengagement is a learned behavior, but so is misguided, non-productive over-involvement.

Reflections

_____

_____

_____

_____

_____

_____

Some people believe holding on and hanging in there are signs of great strength. However, there are times when it takes much more strength to know when to let go and then do it.

— Ann Landers

Jesus said "If any man will come after me, let him deny himself, take up his cross daily, and follow me".

Luke 9:23

DISIDENTIFICATION

Disidentification is difficult. It means letting go of that part of us embedded in the old way. Disidentification leaves us with many painful feelings because a piece of our old self, our heart, is left behind. It sometimes takes years to release it. It takes time for a new identity to develop. The process is slow and often chaotic. But no transition is complete until our identity is fully in the new paradigm.

REFLECTIONS

_____

_____

_____

_____

_____

_____

Life can only be understood backwards; but it must be lived forwards.
— Søren Kierkegaard

The world and the lusts thereof, pass away, but he that does the will of God abides forever.

1 John 2:17

DISENCHANTMENT

Letting go means giving up the blessings and nurture that we received from the old way. This is hard because human beings are creatures of habit. It is hard to give up what has blessed and nurtured us. We have to let go of the old reality with its assumption, e.g., "this relationship is for life" or "my health will last forever." As strange as it seems, we all tend to have our illusions of permanence. Change and transition mean we have to leave the old reality and open to the formation of the new.

REFLECTIONS

_____

_____

_____

_____

_____

_____

Life is a series of natural and spontaneous changes. Don't resist them; that only creates sorrow. Let reality be reality. Let things flow naturally forward in whatever way they like.

— Lao Tzu

MARCH 13

Behold, I stand at the door and knock. If anyone hears my voice and opens the door, I will come in and commune with him.

Revelation 3:20

DISORIENTATION

Having disengaged, given up our identity, and let go of past enchantments, we find ourselves disorientated. Our actions are detached leaving us confused and insecure. This leads us to a zone of chaos. The zone of chaos is painful. But if we can be creative, we move into the new paradigm. As the process of transition progresses, the zone of chaos decreases. Sadly, this zone of chaos discourages many persons and they never move into transition.

Transition is like a trapeze artist waiting for the new baton. To grasp the new baton he has to let go and be suspended in midair for a few seconds. Only then can the acrobat grasp the new baton. If we do not have the faith to let go, we are condemned to the old reality. Surrender requires the patience, faith, and time to not only go through change, but the more difficult process of transition. Sometimes what looks like chaos could be new opportunities bursting through.

REFLECTIONS

We are products of our past, but we don't have to be prisoners of it.

— Rick Warren

MARCH 14

I [Wisdom] was there. . .
when he assigned to the sea its limit,
so that the waters might not transgress his command,
when he marked out the foundations of the earth.

Proverbs 8:29

AFFILIATION AND DIFFERENTIATION

In life, the delicate balance between affiliation and differentiation is often upset. That imbalance affects our boundaries and relationships with others. Without strong boundaries, it is difficult to achieve differentiation. There is a breakdown between that which is us and that which is not us when we want to please, be liked, and fuse with people and problems around us. In so doing, we develop a kind of martyr complex. The idea is that by pleasing or tying to be perfect, we will be loved or admired. That is how we become codependent.

REFLECTIONS

_____

_____

_____

_____

_____

_____

When people show you their boundaries ("I can't do this for you") you feel rejected...part of your struggle is to set boundaries to your own love. Only when you are able to set your own boundaries will you be able to acknowledge, respect and even be grateful for the boundaries of others.

— Henri J.M. Nouwen

MARCH 15

I have fought the good fight, I have finished the race, I have kept the faith.

2 Timothy 4:7

THE ACID TEST OF LOVE

Powerful and highly destructive, shame is the opposite of compassion. The deeper the shame core, the deeper the lack of compassion for ourselves and others. Compassion is not just a feeling. It is being pricked so deeply by the pain of another that we are propelled into action to meet their needs. In compassion there is no *other*. If you hurt, I hurt. If I hurt, you hurt. Our compassion can only be as deep as our love. Love without compassion is sentimentality and the acid test of love is compassion for one's neighbor, for community.

REFLECTIONS

_____

_____

_____

_____

_____

_____

Our human compassion binds us the one to the other - not in pity or patronizingly, but as human beings who have learnt how to turn our common suffering into hope for the future.

— Nelson Mandela

MARCH 16

Be not dismayed for I am thy God.

Isaiah 41:10

ALONE WITH THE ALONE

The journey from *loneliness to solitude* involves opening our hearts to the love that never lets us go and the face which never turns away. Loneliness is increasing in our culture. Studies show that all of us have fewer intimate relationships to share the deep feelings of our hearts than just ten years ago. Loneliness destroys community and leads us to the impersonal crowd.

In solitude we are alone with the *Alone*. Speaking of this, David says, "My soul waits in silence for you and you alone" (Ps. 62:1). Isaiah opens us to the victory of solitude, "Fear thou not, for I am with thee. Be not dismayed for I am thy God" (Isa. 41:10 KJV). Nurtured in solitude, we are prepared for community.

REFLECTIONS

_____

_____

_____

_____

_____

_____

In order to understand the world, one has to turn away from it on occasion.

— Albert Camus

MARCH 17

Do not neglect hospitality, because through it some have entertained
angels without knowing it.

Hebrews 13:2

HEARTS OF HOSPITALITY

Our underlying shame core periodically erupts into anger.
We are often the object of our own anger. Anger is either
internalized or projected onto others. It is in solitude that we
are healed and lovingly moved from *hostility to hospitality.*
Sadly, we often nurture our hostility leaving no space for the
expression of the true self. Even where we are...*we* are what is
missing! Emptying our hearts of hurt, fear, and anger is a
grieving process that opens the door to intimacy.

Because of our losses, many of us live at the hostility pole
which halts our spiritual journey. Anger or hostility may
empower us temporarily, but it blocks us from opening the
doors of our hearts to the love around us. On the other hand, if
we could grieve our losses, we would open to a deeper love than
we have ever known before. As a result, our hearts would
overflow with love and hospitality instead of being incubators
for anger and hostility.

REFLECTIONS

_____

_____

_____

_____

_____

_____

The word 'hospitality' in the New Testament comes from two Greek
words. The first word means 'love' and the second word means
'strangers.' It's a word that means love of strangers.

— Nancy Leigh DeMoss

MARCH 18

We love [God] because he first loved us.

I John 4:19

FIRST LOVE

Stuck in the illusion of our false selves, we drown in selfishness or narcissism. We become attached to our possessions, bow to our idolatries, gratify our consumerism, and yield to our addictions. Hearts open to God's love melt away the illusions of the false self and shame allowing us to experience our true identity as the *beloved of God*. The true self exists only in God and it is there that we live in the awareness of the presence of God. God is love and he loves us to the uttermost. Love is the antidote of shame that makes us lovable and loving.

God's love, our first love, is eternal, unconditional, and redemptive. It anchors us in the kingdom of God. All other loves are temporary, conditional, often disappointing. Secondary loves set us adrift in a temporal sea of illusory perspective. The true self cannot live outside the presence of God's love. Even so, we readily leave his presence and live out of the false self, trapped in busy schedules and urgent time pressures without the awareness of his love.

REFLECTIONS

_____

_____

_____

_____

_____

_____

How on earth are you ever going to explain in terms of chemistry and physics so important a biological phenomenon as first love?

— Albert Einstein

Many waters cannot quench love; rivers cannot wash it away. If one were to give all the wealth of his house for love, it would be utterly scorned.

Song of Solomon 8:7

BELOVED OF GOD

The Last Supper draws its intimacy from Jesus' expressions of love as he experienced them from the Father. Declaring his deep love for them, Jesus said to his disciples, "As the Father has loved me, so have I loved you" (John 15:9). Intimacy emanates from love and our Lord reminds us that his love reaches out to us at the most despairing and difficult points of life.

Regardless of how much we may have failed, how far we have fallen or how much we feel like outcasts, Jesus reminds us that we are the *beloved of God*. Opening to the deep love of God melts away our false self and our shame and restores the true meaning of our identity in God. Our small *i* is swallowed up by the great *I Am*. As a result, we live in God and he lives in us.

REFLECTIONS

_____

_____

_____

_____

_____

_____

*The Last Supper illustrates eight qualities which help guide us in our spiritual journey toward authenticity; the first is **love**.*

— David F. Allen

MARCH 20

COMMUNION

Communion with God always involves silence. Opening ourselves to interior silence creates stillness and in stillness we sit and dine at the table set for two. Experiencing communion with God in silence is a discipline, a learning experience. David said, "I have learned to still and quiet my soul.... Like a weaned child is my soul within me" (Ps. 131:2). In the silence of contemplation, we open ourselves to the naked love of God's presence which bathes our souls and creates the deepest form of intimacy and communion. Communion is enhanced by gratitude. When we are grateful, we give our deepest self. Gratitude is an appreciation that we are the *beloved of God*.

REFLECTIONS

_____

_____

_____

_____

_____

_____

*The Last Supper illustrates eight qualities which help guide us in our spiritual journey toward authenticity; the second is **communion**.*

— David F. Allen

But love your enemies, do good to them and lend to them without expecting to get anything back. Then your reward will be great, and you will be children of the Most High, because he is kind to the ungrateful and wicked.

Luke 6:35

RESISTANCE

Self-destruction is one of the most common ways that we create distance in our lives while at the same time destroying intimacy with God, others, and ourselves. Countering this, Jesus admonishes us to love our enemies. It is God's love that breaks down our resistance to intimacy. It allows us to face the hardened parts of our hearts and experience the deep healing of God's love.

REFLECTIONS

_____

_____

_____

_____

_____

_____

*The Last Supper illustrates eight qualities which help guide us in our spiritual journey toward authenticity; the third is **resistance**.*

— David F. Allen

March 22

Take my yoke upon you and learn from me, for I am gentle and humble in heart, and you will find rest for your souls.

Matthew 11:29

Humility

Humility is the building block of spirituality and the enemy of shame. It always leads to intimacy. Humility is facing the truth about who we are, learning to accept ourselves as we are, not as we would like to be or should be. The road to humility is paved with multiple humiliations. Recognizing the magnificence and holiness of God is more sincerely humbling than focusing on the degradation we have suffered. Taking off his outer garment, our Lord put on the garment of a slave to serve his disciples by washing their feet. When we open to God's love, God exposes our prejudices, superior attitudes, competitive jealousies, and alienating tendencies. We have to be willing to let them go.

Reflections

_____

_____

_____

_____

_____

_____

*The Last Supper illustrates eight qualities which help guide us in our spiritual journey toward authenticity; the fourth is **humility.***

— David F. Allen

March 23

Blessed are the pure in heart, for they will see God.

Matthew 5:8

Simplicity

Our Lord took a basin of water to wash his disciples' feet. At its heart, life is simple. Simplifying our lives in this very complex society is easier said than done. But if we are to make the journey without shame, we have to travel lighter. This requires making some very hard choices. The opportunities to simplify our lives seem to occur at specific times. If we do not take advantage of these opportunities, we may find ourselves experiencing an even greater sense of complexity.

Nothing is more painful than recognizing that we are caught up in the vortex of the hustle and bustle of life. We run around in circles to defend against our shame without the time or space to be present to ourselves or to God. Sadly, we all have experienced this reality pushing us further away from God, the figure and ground of our being.

Reflections

_____

_____

_____

_____

_____

_____

*The Last Supper illustrates eight qualities which help guide us in our spiritual journey toward authenticity; the fifth is **simplicity**.*

— David F. Allen

MARCH 24

"Now that I, your Lord and Teacher, have washed your feet, you also should wash one another's feet".

John 13:14

SERVICE

Dressed as a servant, our Lord bowed and washed his disciples' feet. What a paradox, the almighty and holy God washing the feet of ordinary, lowly human beings. This and this alone is God's love, providing a beautiful picture of intimacy. Though the Lord God is high and mighty, his love is always bent towards those who are humble and contrite. This foot washing demonstrates the love which never fails us. It is a love which reminds us that Christ still washes our feet by sending us friends to encourage us, children to admire us, and spouses to love us.

REFLECTIONS

_____

_____

_____

_____

_____

_____

*The Last Supper illustrates eight qualities which help guide us in our spiritual journey toward authenticity; the sixth is **service**.*

— David F. Allen

MARCH 25

If I go up to the heavens, you are there; if I make my bed in the depths, you are there.

Psalm 139:8

TRANSCENDENCE AND IMMANENCE

Jesus is the lover who always seeks the beloved, he always comes for us. The tragedy is that because of the busyness in our lives, the fatigue in our hearts, and the resistance in our minds, we are often unaware of his presence. This is why we say, "Stop and smell the roses." A rose is a statement from God, blooming and booming in his loving voice that we are loved. As we open our hearts to the transcendent and imminent presence of God, we begin to see his presence in everything around us. He is in the roses, children, friends, lovers, and all of life. The ordinary becomes the bearer of the extraordinary

REFLECTIONS

_____

_____

_____

_____

_____

_____

*The Last Supper illustrates eight qualities which help guide us in our spiritual journey toward authenticity; the seventh is **transcendence**.*

— David F. Allen

Remember how the LORD your God led you all the way in the wilderness these forty years, to humble and test you in order to know what was in your heart.

Deuteronomy 8:2

REMEMBRANCE

Human beings are prone to forgetfulness. Not that we intend to forget, but with all of the stresses and strains of modern life, it is difficult to remain focused. Our internal shame core with the accumulated hurt from our ancestral heritage and personal experience covers or occludes much of the positive in life. We are then left to feast on only the negative. Negative thoughts produce a paralyzing internal addictive dialogue that distracts us from our true essence. As a result, we forget many a hard earned victory, beautiful experiences, and serendipitous moments of life.

REFLECTIONS

_____

_____

_____

_____

_____

_____

*The Last Supper illustrates eight qualities which help guide us in our spiritual journey toward authenticity; the eighth is **remembrance**.*

— David F. Allen

MARCH 27

This is my body which is broken for you.

1 Corinthians 11:24

THE SACRAMENT OF BREAD AND WINE

Jesus recognizes our human tendency to forget and so he instituted a special feast of remembrance the night before his death. Our Lord took the bread, blessed it and broke it. Then Jesus took the cup of wine and, to paraphrase his words, said, "This is my blood shed for the healing of the human heart." In this simple, but profoundly transcendent space-time moment, the mystery of the Eucharist was instituted. My professional experience of the deep shame of addicts in the culture of death and destruction in the world of crack cocaine has created a deeper need for the Eucharist. My only hope of living with the pain of the daily tragedy that I face each day with my clients is the simple mystery of Christ that comes to us in the sacrament of the Eucharist.

REFLECTIONS

When you remember me it means you have carried something of who I am with you, that I have left some mark of who I am on who you are. It means that you can summon me back to your mind even though countless years and miles may stand between us. It means that if we meet again, you will know me. It means that even after I die, you can still see my face and hear my voice and speak to me in your heart.

— Frederick Buechner

MARCH 28

I tell you the truth; I will not drink again of the fruit of the vine until that day when I drink it anew in the kingdom of God.

Mark 14:25

DELIVERED FROM GUILT AND SHAME

The Eucharist is our reminder of the perceptual shift God made on our behalf at Calvary. It was there that he delivered us from the shame of death and destruction. In its place we experience mystical union with our Lord and all his saints. In spite of ever-present death, the Eucharist teaches us that life is full of epiphanies of resurrection. The Eucharist is a prophetic witness to the bright hope of the future beyond this life.

REFLECTIONS

_____

_____

_____

_____

_____

_____

A Sacrament is when something holy happens. It is transparent time, time which you can see through to something deep inside time...at such milestone moments as seeing a baby baptized or being baptized yourself, confessing your sins, getting married, dying, you are apt to catch a glimpse of the almost unbearable preciousness and mystery of life.

— Frederick Buechner

Father, forgive them for they do not know what they are doing.

Luke 23:34

THE FIRST WORD

In the Lord's Prayer, Jesus taught his disciples that God's forgiveness of us is related to us forgiving others. In his pain and agony, Jesus asked his Father to forgive his persecutors. Forgiveness is the only process in life that can reach back into time and heal a wound from events which cannot be changed. As shame-prone persons, we need to forgive ourselves and those who hurt us. Forgiveness releases the prisoner from his cell. The prisoner is us!

Our Lord said, "Forgive them for they do not know what they are doing." Ignorance is not an excuse for cruelty, but many of our deepest wounds are inflicted by people who said or did things in ignorance. The release or elimination of our shame requires forgiveness.

One of the defining characteristics of liberation from the pain of shame is the courage to forgive. Forgiveness is a process, not an isolated event. Forgiveness is not forgetting, it is disconnecting from our shame experiences. Through forgiveness our shame experiences come to consciousness, leaving what were shame-producing memories as mere empty shells devoid of painful feelings.

REFLECTIONS

_____

_____

_____

_____

_____

_____

The cross is the symbol of Christ's passion, that is, his suffering. But in a deeper way, his cross is symbolic of our crosses.

— David F. Allen

Woman, here is your son; and...here is your mother.

John 19:26-27

THE SECOND WORD

There is no more piercing pain in a mother's heart than the tortured death of her child. Mary, the Blessed Virgin, chosen to give birth to the Son of God, was a person of deep thought and contemplation: "Mary treasured up all these things and pondered them in her heart" (Luke 2:19).

We can only imagine the wrenching pain and terrifying agony portrayed in Mary's face as her son hung on the cross. Pain makes us self-absorbed and turns us in upon ourselves and away from others. In contrast, our Lord's love for his mother was deeply internalized and transcended his pain.

Jesus invited his mother into the reality and pathos of his suffering. He recognized the depth and pain of her suffering. He asked the disciple John to take his mother into his home and care for her. In the depth of his own suffering, Jesus reached out in compassion and empathy to his dear mother. In doing so he offered love to us all.

REFLECTIONS

_____

_____

_____

_____

_____

_____

The crucifixion is filled with mystery and represents the shame and brokenness of the human condition.

— David F. Allen

MARCH 31

I tell you the truth, today you will be with me in paradise.

Luke 23:43

THE THIRD WORD

Jesus was crucified between two thieves. Sneering at Jesus from the shame of pride and arrogance, one of the thieves challenged our Lord to do a miracle and save them all. The other thief, speaking from his brokenness, said, "Lord, remember me when you come into your kingdom." It was to the latter that our Lord said the profound and comforting words "Today you will be with me in paradise."

The word *paradise* is Persian and means *walled garden.*[5] When a Persian king honored his subjects, he chose them to walk in the garden with him as companions. Our Lord offered the penitent thief more than immortality; he promised him the honor of being his companion in the Garden of the Courts of Heaven.

REFLECTIONS

_____

_____

_____

_____

_____

_____

Our disjointed lives, wounded hearts, and overwhelmed spirits are awed as we contemplate in silence the passion and brokenness in these seven last words of our Lord.

— David F. Allen

APRIL

The longer I live, the more I realize the impact of attitude on life. Attitude, to me, is more important than facts. It is more important than the past, the education, the money, than circumstances, than failure, than successes, than what other people think or say or do. It is more important than appearance, giftedness or skill. It will make or break a company... a church... a home. The remarkable thing is we have a choice everyday regarding the attitude we will embrace for that day. We cannot change our past... we cannot change the fact that people will act in a certain way. We cannot change the inevitable. The only thing we can do is play on the one string we have, and that is our attitude. I am convinced that life is 10% what happens to me and 90% of how I react to it. And so it is with you... we are in charge of our Attitudes.

— Chuck Swindoll

APRIL 1

Eloi, Eloi, lama sabachthani.

Matthew 27:46

THE FOURTH WORD

"My God, my God, why have you forsaken me?" Piercing and gut wrenching, these words reverberate in the deepest part of the soul. We can all attest to times when heaven was silent and the words of even the most faithful person seemed irrelevant. But our hope and comfort is that our Lord identifies with our dark night of God's absence. He experienced the shame triangle of abandonment, rejection, and humiliation. He gives us courage to face our own shame when our faith runs dry and help eludes us. Walking our hurt trail and bearing our shame, our Lord gives us the courage to make the perceptual shift, to live in love.

REFLECTIONS

_____

_____

_____

_____

_____

The brokenness of the cross is a portal through which our healing and wholeness flows.

— David F. Allen

I thirst.

John 19:28

THE FIFTH WORD

The body is over seventy percent water and without water, life is impossible. Arid and dry are synonymous with thirst and emptiness. The Holy Spirit is the water of life and Jesus promised that if we trust him, our hearts will overflow with living water. But on the cross, rejected by the very Holy Spirit who united him with his Father, the eternal well is dry and Christ cries, "I thirst."

So often the Christ in us thirsts because of our rebellion and disobedience and we give him sour vinegar to drink. He has poured out himself for us; we in turn need to open our hearts in praise and thanksgiving, to let his living water flow through us.

REFLECTIONS

_____

_____

_____

_____

_____

_____

Thou O Lord art the foutain of life...come, drink and be healed.

— David F. Allen

APRIL 3

It is finished.

John 19:30

THE SIXTH WORD

At this cry the temple veil was torn and the work of redemption was complete making the Holiest of Holies accessible to us. Earth is united with heaven and fear dethroned. Love wins and hope springs eternal in our breast as we open to the reality of God's will being done on earth as in heaven.

REFLECTIONS

_____

_____

_____

_____

_____

_____

No one really knows why they are alive until they know what they'd die for.

— Martin Luther King, Jr.

APRIL 4

Father, into your hands I commit my spirit.

Luke 23:46

THE SEVENTH WORD

As he died, our Lord committed his Spirit to God. It is comforting to know that when we come to the end of our journey, God receives our spirit. But we must choose to commit. Jesus lived and died in commitment to God. O God, help us to live and die like our Lord. Through his cross and resurrection, you have freed us to both live and die.

Here is the ultimate act of surrender – letting go and letting God. Our Lord is teaching us about life and death. Since death is a part of life, we can only move beyond our shame if we surrender day by day, and hour by hour to the Love that never lets us go and the Face that never turns away.

REFLECTIONS

_____

_____

_____

_____

_____

_____

And we wept that one so lovely should have a life so brief.
— William Cullen Bryant

April 5

If Christ has not been raised, our preaching is useless and so is your faith.... And if Christ has not been raised...you are still in your sin [shame]. If only for this life we have hope in Christ, we are to be pitied more than all men.

I Corinthians 15:14, 17, 19

Resurrection

The resurrection of Christ completes the sacrificial journey of our Lord to overcome human sin and shame. The resurrection is not a peripheral phenomenon. It is the central point of our Lord's redemptive mission of love to heal the shame of the human condition.

Coming full circle, the resurrection fulfills God's promise to Adam and Eve. God foretold in Genesis 3:15 that the seed of the serpent (Satan) will bruise the heel of their seed, but their seed will crush the serpent's head bringing an end to shame, sin, and the culture of death and destruction.

Reflections

_____

_____

_____

_____

_____

_____

The fact that life and death are 'not two' is extremely difficult to grasp, not because it is so complex, but because it is so simple.

— Ken Wilber

APRIL 6

And behold, a woman of the city, who was a sinner, when she learned that he was reclining at table in the Pharisee's house, brought an alabaster flask of ointment and standing behind him at his feet, weeping, she began to wet his feet with her tears and wiped them with the hair of her head and kissed his feet and anointed them with the ointment.

Luke 7:37-38

MARY MAGDALENE WAS CONNECTED

As a follower of Jesus, Mary experienced a deep connection with our Lord who liberated her from the web of shame and destruction. In Christ her Ego Addictive False Self and shame melted away producing deep healing that allowed her to experience her true identity as the *beloved of God*. In *her* story, we see *our* story in the meaning of the resurrection. It is the story of a broken life that finds healing through an intimate connection to our Lord. It is a journey from wounds to worship. As Thomas Merton said "make ready for the Christ, whose smile like lightening, sets free the song of everlasting glory that now sleeps in your paper flesh".

REFLECTIONS

_____

_____

_____

_____

_____

_____

*Mary Magdalene was **called to connection.***

—David F. Allen

APRIL 7

But standing by the cross of Jesus were his mother and his mother's sister, Mary the wife of Clopas, and Mary Magdalene.

John 19:25

MARY MAGDALENE WAS COMMITTED

True connection always leads to deep commitment. Remaining at the cross during the crucifixion, braving the jeers of the Roman soldiers, Mary demonstrated deep love and commitment. Unlike Pilate, Peter, Judas, and so many of us, Mary was no fair weather friend. True to her convictions, her love was real and no fear, danger, or opposition would deter her from that commitment to her Lord.

After the ghastly experience of witnessing the crucifixion, Mary went to the tomb looking for the body of Jesus despite obvious danger. She went before dawn on the first day of the week. Mary Magdalene demonstrated that our ability to grasp the meaning of the resurrection depends on the depth of our personal commitment.

REFLECTIONS

_____

_____

_____

_____

_____

_____

*Mary Magdalene was **called to commitment.***
—David F. Allen

APRIL 8

Mary Magdalene and Mary the mother of Joses saw where he was laid.

Mark 15:47

MARY MAGDALENE'S CONCERN FOR THE BODY OF CHRIST

Take note in these meditations on Mary Magdalene's life, how she cares for the body of Christ beginning with her first encounter with him in the home of the Pharisee. There she anointed him for death. In the scripture text for today, it is recorded that she sees where they laid his body. Later, in her distress she laments to the angels, to the disciples, and to Jesus himself, who she mistakes for the gardener, that "they have taken his body and I do not know where they have laid him." Finally, she is seen clinging to the risen body of Christ and does not want to let go.

REFLECTIONS

_____

_____

_____

_____

_____

*Mary Magdalene was **called to care for the body of Christ.***

— David F. Allen

Early on the first day of the week, while it was still dark, Mary Magdalene went to the tomb and saw that the stone had been removed from the entrance.

John 20:1

MARY MAGDALENE WAS CALLED TO LOVE

The Gospel of Mark tells us that "Mary Magdalene, Mary the mother of James, and Salome bought spices, so that they might go and anoint him." These women were extremely close to Jesus and loved him dearly. All three had witnessed the crucifixion, risking their lives to be with the one they loved. They were rewarded with the first evidence of the resurrection, the empty tomb.

Love enables us to see with the eyes of the heart. The eyes of love are able to know others beyond physical appearance. St. Francis de Sales wrote long ago, *cor ad cor loquitur,* "heart speaks to heart." Relationship provides an empathic connection allowing us to know the mind and thought of others. Mary and John loved Jesus in a way that gave them that *heart-to-heart* insight on the interpretation of the meaning of his life, death, and resurrection.

REFLECTIONS

_____

_____

_____

_____

_____

_____

*Mary Magdalene was **called to love.***
— David F. Allen

APRIL 10

So she ran and went to Simon Peter and the other disciple, the one whom Jesus loved, and said to them, "They have taken the Lord out of the tomb, and we do not know where they have laid him."

John 20:2

MARY MAGDALENE WAS IN COMMUNITY

To Mary's surprise, the stone at the entrance of the tomb was moved. Excited and afraid, she ran to tell Peter and the other disciples. She was not a loner. She had a sense of community and, thinking the body of Jesus had been stolen, she turned to those who shared her love for Christ.

Community is important in the life of faith. We cannot go it alone. Community supports us and most of all enables us to find guidance in knowing the will of God. The resurrection enhances community, exposes our limitations, vulnerabilities, and woundedness, but it also showers us with grace, understanding, and forgiveness. How can different races get together? How can men and women have long-term relationships? Such unions can only succeed if there is a base for mutual forgiveness and love. We are admonished to forgive each other as God has forgiven us.

REFLECTIONS

*Mary Magdalene was **called to community**.*

— David F. Allen

So Peter and the other disciple started for the tomb. Both were running, but the other disciple outran Peter and reached the tomb first.... Finally the other disciple, who had reached the tomb first, also went inside. He saw and believed. (They still did not understand from Scripture that Jesus had to rise from the dead.) Then the disciples went back to where they were staying.

John 20:3-4, 8-10

MARY MAGDALENE PERSEVERED

Mary anxiously told Peter and "the disciple whom Jesus loved" what she had found at the tomb. Upon hearing the news, both Peter and the other disciple ran to the tomb. The disciple whom Jesus loved arrived first at the tomb and looked in while Peter charged ahead and found the linen wrappings. The other disciple then went inside and found what Peter had seen. The Scriptures say that upon seeing this "the disciple whom Jesus loved" believed.

What we do know is that Mary persisted, she stayed at the tomb. Persistence enhances faith and vice versa. In fact, many times faith just means "keeping on keeping on," "standing firm," or "holding on." As exemplified by Mary, faith means taking the risk of being persistent when others leave us, when our pseudo gods are gone, and we are left alone with the one true God.

REFLECTIONS

_____

_____

_____

_____

_____

_____

*Mary Magdalene was **called to courageous perseverance.***
— David F. Allen

APRIL 12

Then the disciples went back to where they were staying.

John 20:10

THE DISCIPLES' TRANSITION TO A NEW REALITY

We turn for a moment from Mary Magdalene to the two male disciples who returned "to where they were staying" after they rushed to see for themselves the empty tomb. The "Good News" was that Jesus was alive; the bad news was fear of the religious leaders who would accuse them of stealing his body. They retreated to the safety and comfort of home, a place where they were sheltered from the effects of this wonderful but fearful new reality.

Home is familiar and sometimes we live in the prison of the familiar. Afraid, unsure, apprehensive, we drift toward the known. How many of us have lost great opportunities or have even turned away from potential greatness because we were unable to leave the prison of the familiar? There are good reasons to return home, but then we must not let the safety of the familiar prevent us from making the transition to a new reality. For the disciples, that new reality was that Jesus was alive.

REFLECTIONS

_____

_____

_____

_____

_____

_____

Will power does not change men. Time does not change men. Christ does.

— Henry Drummond

Now Mary stood outside the tomb crying. As she wept, she bent over to look into the tomb and saw two angels in white, seated where Jesus' body had been, one at the head and the other at the foot. They asked her, "Woman, why are you crying?" "They have taken my Lord away," she said, "and I don't know where they have put him."

John 20:11-13

MARY MAGDALENE WEPT AT THE TOMB

She not only persisted in staying by the tomb – she stood there weeping. As she wept, she kept looking into the tomb. She mourned for her Lord. She missed him. She wanted to be with him. Mourning means crying in our heart for those we love. We are promised that if we seek him, we shall find him. We are told that those who mourn will be comforted (Matt. 5:4) and, sure enough, as Mary mourned, she saw angels. They asked her why she was weeping. She replied, "They have taken away my Lord … and I do not know where they have put him" (John 20:13).

REFLECTIONS

_____

_____

_____

_____

_____

_____

The Lord's mercy often rides to the door of our heart upon the black horse of affliction.

— Charles H. Spurgeon

APRIL 14

At this, she turned around and saw Jesus standing there, but she did not realize that it was Jesus. He asked her, "Woman, why are you crying? Who is it you are looking for?" Thinking he was the gardener, she said, "Sir, if you have carried him away, tell me where you have put him, and I will get him."

John 20:14-15

MARY MAGDALENE LOOKS BUT DOES NOT YET SEE

Faith and an intense desire for God lead to sight. As someone has said, "Moses saw the burning bush. And the bush still burns, but only those who have eyes can see it." Mary focused on the tomb, unaware of the person standing behind her. The pain of death can be so powerful that the grave becomes our focus. Mary turned and saw a man who asked, "Why are you weeping? Whom are you seeking?" These are poignant questions. Christ confronts the motivation of the heart and questions us about our feelings. He challenges us about what we seek.

REFLECTIONS

_____

_____

_____

_____

_____

_____

When the doors of perception are cleansed, man will see things as they truly are, Infinite.

— William Blake

Jesus said to her, "Mary." She turned toward him and cried out in Aramaic, "Rabboni!" (which means "Teacher").

John 20:16

MARY MAGDALENE HEARD JESUS CALL HER NAME

Jesus called Mary by her name. What a touching moment. Faith has many common components, but above all it is personal. It is being called by one's own name. Each one of us is unique. We each have our own strengths, issues, and vocation. We have been called to be missionaries to our own hearts.

When we lack a clear identity, we are reticent about our personal calling. We feel as if we are nothing but a face in the crowd. We look to someone else to validate our experience. Mary Magdalene had been just an ordinary woman who had spent much of her life in disgrace. She miraculously found her way to the *Holy Other*, to the cross, and to the tomb in the darkness of that first Easter morning.

REFLECTIONS

_____

_____

_____

_____

_____

_____

*Mary Magdalene was **called by her name**.*

— David F. Allen

Jesus said, "Do not hold on to me, for I have not yet ascended to the Father. Go instead to my brothers and tell them, 'I am ascending to my Father and your Father, to my God and your God.'" [18] Mary Magdalene went to the disciples with the news: "I have seen the Lord!" And she told them that he had said these things to her.

John 20:17-18

MARY MAGDALENE HAS A MESSAGE FOR THE WORLD

Mary Magdalene's experience of celebration is intimately connected to her willingness to stay at the cross, to persist at the tomb, to mourn for him. We cannot expect the mountaintop experiences of faith without the valleys of commitment, persistence, and mourning. She was sent: "Go and tell!" Ecstatic, Mary clung to the body of Jesus for which she had been looking. She wanted to stay with him forever. But Jesus told her, "Go to my brothers and tell them, 'I am returning to my Father and your Father, to my God and your God'" (John 20:17).

The joy of knowing Christ is not to exhaust him with our emotion, but to allow him to guide us into his service. He sends us to go and create community. Go to the hungry, the hurting. Go to the imprisoned, the oppressed. Let them know Jesus lives. Tell them that because of the resurrection there is love and there is hope. Mary Magdalene announced the resurrection, first, to her own self, then to her community. Finally, she brings the message of the resurrection to a broken world, that is, to you and to me.

REFLECTIONS

---

*Mary Magdalene was **called to tell others.***

— David F. Allen

April 17

How foolish you are, and how slow of heart to believe in all that the prophets have spoken! Did not the Christ have to suffer these things and then enter his glory?' And beginning with Moses and all the prophets, he explained to them what was said in all the Scriptures concerning himself.

Luke 24:25-27

The Eternal Word

Although the two disciples traveling to Emmaus saw the empty tomb, it was still not clear to them that Christ was alive. The risen Christ met two disciples on the road to Emmaus and confronted them about their resistance to believing the Scripture.

Clearly the Word of God is not optional to the spiritual life; it is an essential building block. For God who has revealed himself in his son has also revealed himself in his Word. As Jesus said, "Heaven and earth will pass away, but my words will never pass away" (Mark 13:31).

Like we ourselves, the disciples were impeded in their ability to see the reality of the resurrection because they did not believe the Scripture. We live in ignorance and fear because we do not take seriously the discipline of studying and understanding and obeying his Word.

Reflections

One of the keys to real religious experience is the shattering realization that no matter how hateful we are to ourselves, we are not hateful to God.

— Thomas Merton

APRIL 18

Be still, and know that I am God. I will be exalted among the nations, I will be exalted in the earth!

Psalm 46:10

CHOOSING SILENCE

An empty room is silent, it has no choice. But a room where people choose not to speak or move is still. Silence is a given, the *silence of stillness* is a gift. As we journey further into interior silence, we open to stillness and a spaciousness of spirit. In the *silence of stillness* we are our true selves and sit at the interior table with God.

REFLECTIONS

_____

_____

_____

_____

_____

_____

The endless cycle of idea and action,
Endless invention, endless experiment,
Brings knowledge of motion, but not of stillness,
Knowledge of speech, but not of silence.

— T. S. Eliot

April 19

God in whom we live, breathe and have our being.

Acts 17:28

Our Existence in God

God is love and, in his presence, our defensive Ego Addictive False Self and shame melt away revealing our true identity as the *beloved of God*. The stillness of silence is not the absence of noise, but the absence of our Ego Addictive False Self blocking us from our true essence in God and the interrelatedness of all things. When we lose touch with inner stillness, we lose touch with ourselves. That inner stillness is where we meet God and it is in him and through him that we have our existence.

Reflections

_____

_____

_____

_____

_____

_____

Two possibilities exist: either we are alone in the Universe or we are not. Both are equally terrifying.

— Arthur C. Clarke

APRIL 20

For now we see in a mirror dimly, but then face to face. Now I know in part; then I shall know fully, even as I have been fully known.

I Corinthians 13:12

RECOGNIZING THE FACE OF JESUS

There are a lot of different ways to be recognized. Sometimes it is impersonal recogition like showing a driver's licence or scanned by facial recognition software. Being recognized by the public is fame without personal knowledge of the other person. To be recognized professionally by your peers is an honor, but implies only that I am known by my work, not who I am. Recognizing an old friend and being recognized in return is a joy because we know and are known by another. The first time a child's face lights up when a parent arrives home or a lover says your name is unforgettable. There is only One who fully knows us and his is the face that never turns away.

REFLECTIONS

_____

_____

_____

_____

_____

_____

You don't forget the face of the person who was your last hope.
— **Suzanne Collins**, *The Hunger Games*

APRIL 21

His name is to be called John.

Luke 1:63

NAMED OUT OF THE SILENCE

Stillness is *knowing* and *being known*. Turning doubt to faith and fear to love, stillness instills courage making our weak legs strong. When the priest Zachariah was told that his wife would have a baby in her old age and his name was to be John, he scoffed in unbelief. How did God get his attention? He shut Zachariah's mouth. He learned silence. When his wife had a child, in the transformation from unbelief to enlightenment, Zachariah wrote, 'His name is to be called John'.

REFLECTIONS

_____

_____

_____

_____

_____

_____

It is true that those we meet can change us, sometimes so profoundly that we are not the same afterwards, even unto our names.
— Yann Martel, *Life of Pi*

APRIL 22

Keep silence and hear, O Israel: this day you have become the people of the Lord your God.

Deuteronomy 27:9

THE SOUNDS OF STILLNESS

Akin to deep listening, stillness is acceptance and obedience. The word *stillness* is derived from the same Latin root *audiens* from which we get *audience,* and creates an intimate connection between listening and obedience. Stillness allows us to listen, obey, and follow the voice of love that speaks so loudly in all areas of life.

The word *absurd* is derived from the Latin root *absurdis* meaning *deafness.* Without stillness, life is absurd because we become deaf to the meaning and beauty of life. Without stillness the voice of love is faint and without the experience of the *Eternal Love,* it is difficult to be aware of God's presence.

REFLECTIONS

Go placidly amid the noise and the haste, and remember what peace there may be in silence.

— Max Ehrmann

April 23

Rejoice always, pray without ceasing, give thanks in all circumstances; for this is the will of God in Christ Jesus for you.

1 Thessalonians 5:16-18

Emanuel is God with Us

Prayer is the discipline of the moment. When we pray we enter into the presence of God whose name is "God with us." To pray is to listen attentively to the one who addresses us here and now. When we dare to trust that we are never alone, that God is always with us, then we can gradually detach ourselves from the voices that make us guilty or anxious. Thus we allow ourselves to remain in the moment with God.

Reflections

_____

_____

_____

_____

_____

_____

To be effective prayers we need to be effective lovers. He prayeth well who loveth well.

— Samuel Coleridge

APRIL 24

Truly, truly, I say to you, unless a grain of wheat falls into the earth and dies, it remains alone; but if it dies, it bears much fruit.

John 12:24

CONTEMPLATION AS SURRENDER

Contemplation is surrender. Surrender is letting go, giving over control of our life from our Ego Addicted False Self. In surrender we move from the fear-based false self to our true, love-based self in God. It is a matter of simple awareness; contemplative prayer is opening to the stillness of silence. Stillness melts away our false self and shame which is based on our social status, our possessions, what we feel and what we do.

In the stillness of contemplation, we experience our true identity as the *beloved of God*. Our most personal, true self is also universal in God. As the *beloved of God*, we open up in relationship to ourselves, to each other, and to God's garden, the world.

REFLECTIONS

_____

_____

_____

_____

_____

_____

I have been driven many times upon my knees by the overwhelming conviction that I had no where else to go. My own wisdom and that of all about me seemed insufficient for that day.

— Abraham Lincon

April 25

When I remember you upon my bed, and meditate on you in the watches of the night.

Psalm 63:6

A World Pregnant with God

We cannot demand the gift of contemplation – union and communion with God. We can only be faithful because God is the giver of all good things including the gift of his presence. The presence of God is not something we choose depending on our will or wish. It is the condition of our very existence.

When we become aware of the presence of God's love and willingly turn towards it, it becomes real and life changing. All things become new, he is near to all who seek him. As a result, the world becomes pregnant with God and life and the outpouring of his grace and love.

Reflections

Earth's crammed with heaven,
And every wild bush alive with God,
And only he who sees takes off his shoes:
The rest sit 'round and pluck blackberries.
— Elizabeth Barrett Browning

Beloved, let us love one another, for love is from God, and whoever loves has been born of God and knows God.

1 John 4:7

THE TRANSFORMATION OF CONSCIOUSNESS

Contemplation is the transformation of consciousness in which we discover our true identity as the *beloved of God* and live in the constant awareness of his love, mission, and healing presence in the world. Contemplation manifests itself through prayer, personal growth, relationships, work, appreciation of beauty, and compassionate service to others. Contemplation is a commitment to the vision of God's love and to the mission of his love in the world.

REFLECTIONS

_____

_____

_____

_____

_____

_____

True prayer is nothing but love.

— St. Augustine

By this all people will know that you are my disciples, if you have love for one another.

John 13:35

VISION WITH A MISSION

Vision without the mission of his love is an empty illusion leading to a non-creative self-absorption. The mission without the vision of God's love leads to busyness, burnout, and non-redemptive activity. Contemplation must always be balanced by the vision and the mission of God's love.

Called to a mountain top fellowship with God, Moses had to return to the valley to serve the people. Always leading to compassion within and without, contemplation essentially means going to the mountain top only to return to kneel and wash the feet of our brothers and sisters.

REFLECTIONS

_____

_____

_____

_____

_____

_____

It is in dialogue with others that we are called to life.

— Leanne Payne

APRIL 28

Anyone who does not love does not know God, because God is love.

1 John 4:8

A DEEPER LOVE

Our deepest desires express a hunger that only God can satisfy. Unfortunately, we often give our hearts to that which is not God, such as relationships, addictions, rituals, and possessions. The heart becomes free only by accepting an invitation to deeper love. But because of our narcissistic tendencies, we even use this love to seek ourselves. We need to learn to empty our hearts of all attachments and be filled by God. God's love gives life and slowly transforms us, healing our deepest wounds of shame.

REFLECTIONS

One of the deep secrets of life is that all that is really worth the doing is what we do for others.

— Lewis Carroll

APRIL 29

It is he who made us, and we are his.

Psalm 100:3

COVERT TRANSFORMATION

During our inward journey toward stillness, God transforms us into the image of Christ by breaking down the false self and eliminating shame to give birth to an awareness of the true self in God. The journey is filled with ups and downs because transformation occurs slowly and covertly. As we continue our journey in prayer, we open to the awareness of God's presence, not only at the time of prayer, but also in the hum drum experience of daily life.

In surrender, we are absorbed in the awareness of God and, as a result, our satisfaction is only found in his loving presence. Experiencing the stillness of God's presence and love, we long for it and seek it with a passion.

REFLECTIONS

_____

_____

_____

_____

_____

_____

A talent is formed in stillness, a character in a torrent.

— Johann Wolfgang Goethe

April 30

Shall we accept good from God, and not trouble?

Job 2:10

Come What May

It is easy to say we abandon ourselves to God. But living the abandonment out in practice is the real challenge. We come to realize that God is the dancer and the music in the cosmic dance of the music of love. Knowing God is not all joy, at times it is painful. It is like going to the dentist to prevent tooth decay or jogging for health. The spiritual journey is not a sentimental trip of ecstasy. As God leads and directs our paths, we do not change the world as we know it, but we are changed and so is our vision of the world.

Reflections

_____

_____

_____

_____

_____

We attract what we expect
We reflect what we desire
We become what we expect
We mirror what we desire.
— William A. Ward

MAY

The psychological rule says that when an inner situation is not made conscious, it happens outside, as fate. That is to say, when the individual remains divided and does not become conscious of...inner contradictions, the world must perforce act out the conflict and be torn into opposite halves.

— Carl Jung

MAY 1

Blessed are those who hunger and thirst for righteousness, for they shall be satisfied.

Matthew 5:6

GRIPPED BY DESIRE

We are all familiar with the rationalizations that characterize our lives such as, my work is my prayer, I'm too busy to pray, I just pray when the spirit moves me. Such excuses maintain the status quo and encourage spiritual poverty and lethargy. We are made by God, for God, and nothing less than God will satisfy us. C S. Lewis claimed that he was gripped by a desire that made everything else fade into insignificance. It is clear why the false self is one of the greatest barriers to a prayer life.

REFLECTIONS

_____

_____

_____

_____

_____

_____

Blessed are those in whom grace shines so copiously that love of food does not arouse excessive appetite, but lets them hunger after righteousness.

— Dante, *Divine Comedy*

MAY 2

Then a voice said to him, "What are you doing here, Elijah?"

1 Kings 19:13

SOUNDS OF SILENCE

God tells the prophet to go out and stand on the mountain in the presence of the Lord as he passes by. In contemplation, regardless of our pain, we long for the healing presence of God. Only the presence of God can satisfy the deepest longings of our heart. Then God sent a great wind, but God was not in the wind. There was an earthquake, but God was not in the earthquake. Then there was a fire and God was not in the fire. After the fire there was a sound of silence – stillness, space, the still small voice of God.

REFLECTIONS

_____

_____

_____

_____

_____

_____

It is vanity to wish for long life and to care little about a well-spent life.

— Thomas A' Kempis

For he commanded and raised the stormy wind and lifted up the waves of the sea.

Psalm 107:25

TERRIFYING POWER

I have watched the sea for many hours, but the most disturbing spectacle occurred one day in October, 1991, when a series of tidal waves rushed over the shore. Huge waves crashed fiercely against the seawalls, picking up large boulders as if they were just pebbles. What terrifying power! My heart jumped with fear and awe as I drove along the beach road as quickly as I dared. A huge wave attacked my car, knocking me from side to side. After that I came to respect the sea, and I am beginning to understand why it has been said that those who go down to the sea know the mysteries of God. The thunder of the waves broadcasts the mighty power of the Creator.

REFLECTIONS

_____

_____

_____

_____

_____

_____

A man may lose the good things of this life against his will; but if he loses the eternal blessings, he does so with his own consent.

— St. Augustine

MAY 4

Paul sent for the disciples, and after encouraging them, he said farewell and departed for Macedonia.

THE LONG GOODBYE

The minute we are born we begin the process of saying goodbye. When we leave the womb, we say goodbye to the safety and security of being perfectly fed and nurtured. This is probably the hardest thing we do in our whole life, so it's a good thing we don't remember it! Every goodbye represents a microcosm of our own death. The Last Supper is particularly significant to me because in psychotherapy terms, it was the Lord's "termination session" with His disciples. He wanted to tell them goodbye before He went to his final test, the cross.

REFLECTIONS

_____

_____

_____

_____

_____

_____

No one is useless in this world who lightens the burden of it for anyone else.

— Charles Dickens

May 5

And he said to them, "I have earnestly desired to eat this Passover with you before I suffer."

Luke 22:15

Sweet Communion

Our Lord really wanted to tell his disciples what was going on in his heart at the Last Supper. He was telling them this was the heart of his ministry, the heart of the meaning of his life here on Earth. In other words, "Listen to me carefully because I really want to share with you what my whole purpose in coming to earth was all about." He outlined a memorial sacrament we now call communion that gives life meaning and hope, and leads to life that goes beyond the issues of this world.

Reflections

_____

_____

_____

_____

_____

_____

Have your heart right with Christ, and he will visit you often, and so turn weekdays into Sundays, meals into sacraments, homes into temples, and earth into heaven.

— Charles H. Spurgeon

MAY 6

Now before the Feast of the Passover, when Jesus knew that his hour had come to depart out of this world to the Father, having loved his own who were in the world, he loved them to the end.

John 13:1

THE SUSTAINING POWER OF GOD'S LOVE

The first and basic step to discovery of the true self is love. We must be open to the sustaining power of God's love, the creative, redemptive, healing force of life. It is the nature of the false self to save us from knowing the truth about our real selves, from penetrating the deeper causes of our unhappiness, from seeing ourselves as we really are: vulnerable, afraid, terrified and unable to let our real selves emerge. At the Last Supper Christ made it clear he loved his disciples. He reminded them that regardless of what would happen, God's love would continue to reach out to them. "He loved them to the end."

REFLECTIONS

_____

_____

_____

_____

_____

_____

Only love can be divided endlessly and still not diminish.
— Anne Morrow Lindbergh

MAY 7

For through the Spirit, by faith, we ourselves eagerly wait for the hope of righteousness.

Galatians 5:5

THERE WAS HOPE

When I was looking for a way to help my patients learn to love and be loved, I realized that human love, from a Christian perspective, is based on God's love. And God's love fuels human love. If my patients hadn't received love as children, they could still get it – and give it – by opening their hearts to God's love.

Life then made sense to me. There *was* hope. Even for a child who didn't have a secure family or the love of a mother, God's love for that child was unchallenged. His love could still heal those who would open their hearts to receive that love. And through His love hurting persons could meet other people who could also share His love — and help them.

REFLECTIONS

Every heart sings a song, incomplete, until another heart whispers back. Those who wish to sing always find a song.

— Plato

Take care lest your heart be deceived, and you turn aside and serve other gods and worship them.

Deuteronomy 11:16

WE BECOME OUR OWN GOD

Sometimes it's scary to see how deeply our hearts can be deceived. The issue of godship is a predominant theme in the psychotherapy of behavior. Overwhelmed by circumstances beyond our control, we tend to invest problems with such psychological energy that they usurp the place of worship in our lives and gain gripping power over us. The result is dehumanization, depression, burnout, and in some cases, self-destruction.

The importance of perspective — keeping God, ourselves, and our problems in rightful proportions — is stressed throughout the discovery process. But we live in a world of lost perspective. In our confusion we often focus on ourselves. We become our own god.

REFLECTIONS

_____

_____

_____

_____

_____

_____

A God who lets us prove his existence would be an idol.
— Dietrich Bonhoeffer

And when you pray, you must not be like the hypocrites. For they love to stand and pray in the synagogues and at the street corners, that they may be seen by others.

Matthew 6:5

BALCONY PEOPLE

All around us we find individuals who become what one counselor called "balcony people", people who act out their lives as if they are on stage – with one eye always glancing up to the balcony to see if others are gently applauding. Rather than living by convictions and values, the balcony people's actions are chosen to ensure that others approve, admire, and sympathize. They strive to manipulate their love stories rather than loving from the heart.

Balcony people choose the role – martyr, caregiver, daring adventurer – that most pleases their target audience. Life is ruled by what they think others will think of them. Not surprisingly, balcony people suffer from the constant pressures of "performance anxiety" and self-promotion. They are narcissists.

REFLECTIONS

_____

_____

_____

_____

_____

I've often stood silent at a party for hours listening to my movie idols turn into dull and little people.

— Marilyn Monroe

MAY 10

Pride goes before destruction, and a haughty spirit before a fall.
Proverbs 16:18

THE PRIDE OF NARCISSISM

In Greek, *narkissos,* the name of the beautiful plant with showy yellow or white flowers, is traditionally connected, by virtue of the narcissus plant's narcotic effects, with the word *narke,* meaning "numbness, torpor." Hence the word *narcotic,* a substance that blunts the senses, causes euphoria, and when used habitually can be addictive. Thus, the association of narcissism and addiction is clear from the root of the word.

In psychiatry, a narcissistic personality is "a personality disorder characterized by extreme self-centeredness and self-absorption, fantasies involving unrealistic goals, and excessive need for attention and admiration, and disturbed interpersonal relationships." This inordinate love and preoccupation with oneself is also characterized by a lack of interest and empathy for others — in spite of the pursuit of others to obtain admiration and approval.

REFLECTIONS

Narcissists are too busy proving their worth– or more properly disproving their worthlessness – to feel the love, appreciation and joy of being human.

— S.M. Johnson

MAY 11

But he was pierced for our transgressions; he was crushed for our iniquities; upon him was the chastisement that brought us peace, and with his wounds we are healed.

Isaiah 53:5

WOUNDED PEOPLE

While talking about the wounded inner child is currently in vogue, I prefer to talk about the wounded inner person. I have met many persons who have had a very secure childhood experience and were strongly protected and supported through many painful experiences. But somehow things went bad for them later in life – a broken marriage, a child with great potential who messed up, the death of a loved one, or the abrupt end of a promising career. We are wounded in childhood *and* in adult life.

To compound the problem of the pain in their past, children being raised in our Western culture have come to expect so much materially in life that self-gratification becomes the expected and accepted norm.

REFLECTIONS

May our Lord's sweet hand square us and hammer us, and strike off all kinds of pride, self-love, world-worship, and infidelity, so that He can make us stones and pillars in His Father's house.

— Samuel Rutherford

MAY 12

My beloved speaks and says to me: "Arise, my love, my beautiful one, and come away.

Song of Solomon 2:10

I AM BECAUSE I AM LOVE

Discovery is finding the transcendence of God, love, joy, and inner peace that exist apart from our circumstances. Where there is love there will be pain. The love of Jesus led Him to suffering as well as to joy. He was a Man of Sorrows, familiar with suffering because He cared about us so much. As I reach for God's love, I often ponder the hurt trail of Jesus, the One who was fully God and fully man.

Christ endured this pain because He loved us. We can think of his love as we walk our own painful experiences. In my view, it is impossible to deal with the woundedness in our own lives unless we are entwined in a cocoon of God's love. It is God's love that breaks through the universe and sustains us. It gives us the "I" in our lives, a sense of ourselves and allows us to stand with confidence and say, "I am because I am loved."

REFLECTIONS

_____

_____

_____

_____

_____

_____

Our Lord Jesus Christ, the Word of God, of his boundless love, became what we are that he might make us what he himself is.

— Iranaeus

So God created man in his own image, in the image of God he created him; male and female he created them.

Genesis 1:27

A BLUEPRINT FOR LIVING

Everything in life is created twice – first in the mind of the creator and then in reality. If you're going to build a building, you conceptualize it in your mind, than you make it a reality. We imitate what we have learned by experience – even if that experience is suspect. Whose blueprints are you following in your life? Your mother's? Your father's? Or do you live in a codependent way with society around you?

The love of God in our lives means we are made in His image and therefore we have authority to draw our own blueprints, write our own scripts. In that script we can choose to imitate the model of love Jesus provided for us; we can develop our personal mission statement and then see it created.

REFLECTIONS

_____

_____

_____

_____

_____

_____

Consider how impossible nobility of character would be if our goodness were untried innocence instead of victorious virtue.

— Henry Emerson Fosdick

MAY 14

And he said, "O man greatly loved, fear not, peace be with you; be strong and of good courage." And as he spoke to me, I was strengthened and said, "Let my lord speak, for you have strengthened me."

Daniel 10:19

CREATED FOR COMMUNION

We were created for communion; it's a basic requirement for meaningful human relationships. One meaning of being created in the image of God is that we live in fellowship with others just as the Holy Trinity is a love relationship between the Father, Son, and Holy Spirit. We were not created to be alone, but the wounds inflicted on our souls by those we trusted can drive us into isolation, not solitude, but loneliness.

It is not the pain in childhood that injured our hearts, but the feeling that no one supported us through that pain. Communion – community – gives us support. Community helps us to have the courage to reflect on our painful feelings and then open our hearts to love.

REFLECTIONS

_____

_____

_____

_____

_____

You gain strength, courage and confidence by every experience in which you really stop to look fear in the face.

— Eleanor Roosevelt

MAY 15

By faith he kept the Passover and sprinkled the blood, so that the destroyer of the firstborn might not touch them.

Hebrews 11:28

THE PASSOVER PERSPECTIVE

In the communion of the Last Supper, Christ was sharing much more than a meal with his disciples. It was their last meal together before the test of the cross. It was the Passover feast, a Jewish celebration by which they remembered their miraculous deliverance from Egypt after the sign of the lamb's blood on the door post of their homes had saved them from the angel of death.

Passover represented the identity of the Jews, giving them cohesion, fellowship, community, and hope for the future. From Christ's perspective, it was a time to look forward to what God would do in the future. He knew he would soon have to walk the way of the cross. He was saying, "We are in this together. Regardless of what happens, my love will be stronger than death."

REFLECTIONS

_____

_____

_____

_____

_____

_____

Courage is almost a contradiction in terms. It means a strong desire to live, taking the form of a readiness to die.

— G. K. Chesterton

MAY 16

And after he had taken leave of them, he went up on the mountain to pray.

Mark 6:46

THE HALLMARK OF CHRIST'S MINISTRY

Regardless of how busy our Lord was here on earth, he always took time to spend with God, the Father. This was the hallmark of his ministry. In the midst of meeting people's needs for healing and deliverance, He would arise and depart into the mountains to pray.

Prayer is two-sided. Prayer is the Holy Spirit in us relating to our hearts, and Prayer is God calling us to communion with himself. Prayer completes the circuit between us and God, giving us hope and direction. Prayer is opening our hearts to the prayer of God taking place in our lives.

REFLECTIONS

_____

_____

_____

_____

_____

_____

Prayer makes your heart bigger, until it is capable of containing the gift of God himself.

— Mother Teresa

For thus said the Lord God, the Holy One of Israel, "In repentence and rest you shall be saved; in quietness and in trust shall be your strength."

Isaiah 30:15

RESTING IN THE EVERLASTING ARMS

Sometimes the fearful thoughts whirling in our heads and the noise of life around us are so loud we cannot hear the Spirit praying within us. One person described it this way: "In the early days of my faith, prayer was mostly petition. But in seeking a deep experience of God and the spiritual healing of my inner life, prayer became waiting in the presence of God. The assurance was that He knows what I need. Thus prayer essentially is communion with Him."

REFLECTIONS

_____

_____

_____

_____

_____

_____

When Christ calls a man, he bids him come and die.

— Dietrich Bonheoffer

MAY 18

And when he heard that it was Jesus of Nazareth, he began to cry out and say, "Jesus, Son of David, have mercy on me!"

Mark 10:47

CHRIST PRAYS FOR US

Once we open our hearts to the presence of God, He prays through us. The apostle Paul told the Roman Christians, "the Spirit himself bears witness with our spirit that we are children of God... The Spirit himself makes intercession for us with groanings which cannot be uttered." There are certain things, such as suffering, we don't understand, and prayer allows God to pray through us, to take the deep hurt feelings of our heart away so we can open our hearts to love and joy. I believe Christ prays for us, even when we may not be aware of it.

REFLECTIONS

_____

_____

_____

_____

_____

_____

I have held many things in my hands, and have lost them all; but whatever I have placed in God's hands, that I still possess.

— Martin Luther

MAY 19

You keep him in perfect peace whose mind is stayed on you, because he trusts in you.

Isaiah 26:3

THE DEVELOPMENT OF SELF

Solitude requires the development of the self so one can be nourished by the memories of past meaningful experiences, rather than frantically seeking new experiences. Solitude requires reducing the noise around us to hear the true music of our heart. It means moving beyond the pangs and craving for human contact to listen to the voice of God, or, as someone has said, to hearing the music of angels. Solitude is the deep spiritual awareness that we are the 'beloved child of God'.

REFLECTIONS

A self is not something static, tied up in a pretty parcel and handed to the child finished and complete. A self is always becoming.

— Madeleine L'Engle

MAY 20

Search me, Oh, God and know my heart; test me and know my anxious thoughts. See if there is any offensive way in me, and lead me in the way everlasting.

Ps. 139:23-24

THE HESYCHAST TRADITION

The challenge of prayer is to move beyond the mere intellectual exercise so that prayer comes from the heart. When I was teaching at Yale, Father Henri Nouwen told us of the Hesychast tradition in which the monks repeat the Jesus prayer: "Lord Jesus Christ, Holy Son of God, have mercy upon me." As they repeat it hour after hour, day after day this prayer sinks into their hearts and becomes automatic. Then their prayers become like breathing and occur without ceasing in their waking and sleeping moments.

REFLECTIONS

_____

_____

_____

_____

_____

God whispers to us in our pleasures, speaks in our conscience, but shouts in our pains: it is His megaphone to rouse a deaf world.

— C. S. Lewis

Ascribe to the Lord the glory due his name; worship the Lord in the splendor of holiness.

Psalm 29:2

THE SPLENDOR OF GOD

Enjoying moments of solitude is a sign of true communion with God and ourselves. We become comfortable, as psychiatrists say, "thinking about our feelings and feeling about our thoughts." This communion centers on being rather than doing. It is processing our lives: counting blessings, mourning past mistakes, and simply praying for others. It is meditation on the splendor of God and His creation.

REFLECTIONS

_____

_____

_____

_____

_____

_____

I would rather feel compassion than know the meaning of it.
— Thomas Aquinas

MAY 22

Two are better than one, because they have a good reward for their toil.
For if they fall, one will lift up his fellow. But woe to him who is alone
when he falls and has not another to lift him up!

Ecclesiastes 4:9-10

FOR IF THEY FALL

Such isolation is often rationalized by the need to complete certain tasks associated with our work or the upkeep of our homes. Or we pull back to protect ourselves from the potential others have to hurt us. But isolation is always a symptom of a deeper spiritual problem; our hearts have been blocked to communion by pain. Once we have released that pain, we are ready to consider deep communion as a part of our spiritual discovery.

REFLECTIONS

I do not believe in a fate that falls on men however they act; but I do
believe in a fate that falls on them unless they act.

— G. K. Chesterton

MAY 23

The soul of Jonathan was knit to the soul of David, and Jonathan loved him as his own soul.

1 Samuel 18:1

THE BONDS OF COMMUNION

True spirituality moves beyond self-actualization to the consideration of others. The acid test of communion with God and with the self is a formation of loving community. Take David and Jonathan, for instance; it is said that they loved each other so much their souls were knit together and that "Jonathan made a covenant with David, because he loved him as his own soul." What a friendship!

REFLECTIONS

Friendship is born at that moment when one person says to another: "What! You too? I thought I was the only one."

— C.S. Lewis

MAY 24

For as we share abundantly in Christ's sufferings, so to through Christ we share abundantly in comfort.

2 Corinthians 1:5

SHARING HIS SUFFERING

True spirituality leads to intimate relationships in the development of community – not to withdraw from society. The Last Supper, during which Holy Communion was initiated, is the call for communion and community. As we partake of the body and blood of Christ, we share intimately in His sufferings while at the same time we commit ourselves more deeply to each other in obedience to seeing God's will done on earth.

REFLECTIONS

_____

_____

_____

_____

_____

_____

Our lives begin to end the day we become silent about things that matter.

— Dr. Martin Luther King, Jr.

May 25

He has made everything beautiful in its time. Also, he has put eternity into man's heart.

Ecclesiastes 3:11a

Eternity in Our Hearts

We humans have eternity stamped in our hearts. But this desire for immortality and transcendent meaning can be destroyed by the mundane, so it becomes an illusion, rather than reality. The illusion whispers, things will always be as they are. I can somehow stop the clock and enter eternity unaffected by age or death or the consequence of choice. Tragedy, illness, death, or financial problems unmask the illusion and remind us of the fragile and transitory nature of life.

Reflections

_____

_____

_____

_____

_____

_____

You must live in the present, launch yourself on every wave, find your eternity in each moment. Fools stand on their island of opportunities and look toward another land. There is no other land; there is no other life but this.

— Henry David Thoreau

MAY 26

You will know the truth, and the truth will set you free.

John 8:31-32

A COMMITMENT TO REALITY

There will always be times when doubts and fears come to mind. Discovery is a commitment to the reality of life, which allows us to acknowledge our emotions to God and ourselves in a direct manner. No pretending. No hiding. No berating ourselves because of honest emotions. We simply tell God how we feel in our confusion and hurt, asking him to reassure and comfort us. Then, with our hearts laid open before him, we can approach the Bible with eyes to see and ears to hear.

REFLECTIONS

_____

_____

_____

_____

_____

_____

Face reality as it is, not as it was or as you wish it to be.

— Jack Welch

So we do not lose heart. Though our outer self is wasting away, our inner self is being renewed day by day.

2 Corinthians 4:16

DISCOURAGING VOICES

Resistance can also occur when powerful feelings of anger, bitterness, guilt, and discouragement give rise to voices of shame from our past:

- You're not good enough.
- You are a failure.
- Life never goes your way.
- You can't get ahead.
- Nobody cares about you.
- Why bother? You'll never succeed anyway.

How powerful these voices are, discouraging even the strongest saints. Love is the antidote to shame. When these antidotes occur, practice resting in the love of God.

REFLECTIONS

_____

_____

_____

_____

_____

_____

Never discourage anyone...who continually makes progress, no matter how slow.

— Plato

If we confess our sins, he is faithful and just to forgive us our sins and to cleanse us from all unrighteousness.

1 John 1:9

FREE OF GUILT

Guilt is a particularly powerful force especially in the lives of individuals who have gone through a recovery process. Often there is a gap between what they expect of themselves and their actual behavior in times of trouble. Guilt occurs when one relapses or fails to live up to one's own standards. It adds unnecessary burdens to an already stressful ordeal. But true guilt can be cleansed from the conscience in a matter of moments through repentance and prayers of confession.

REFLECTIONS

_____

_____

_____

_____

_____

_____

To be a Christian means to forgive the inexcusable because God has forgiven the inexcusable in you.

— C.S. Lewis

*But when he was **accused** by the chief priests and elders, he gave no answer.*

Matthew 27:12

FALSE GUILT

False guilt is a psychological phenomenon that must be countered by truth. Our hypersensitive consciences stand ready to accuse us at the least sign of anticipated, exaggerated, or actual relapse into wrongdoing. This creates such rigidity that we often topple under the sheer weight of unrealistic expectations. False guilt leaves us weary and depressed because at every point of resistance we assume too much responsibility for others and our circumstances. We automatically assume that we are at fault.

REFLECTIONS

_____

_____

_____

_____

_____

_____

I prefer to be true to myself, even at the hazard of incurring the ridicule of others, rather than to be false, and to incur my own abhorrence.

— Frederick Douglass

MAY 30

Therefore, preparing your minds for action, and being sober-minded, set your hope fully on the grace that will be brought to you at the revelation of Jesus Christ.

1 Peter 1:13

AMAZING GRACE

An antidote to fear and the powerful obstacles placed in our path to wholeness is a childlike, trusting faith in God's love. Simple faith, no bigger than a mustard seed, allows us to walk in grace, rather than in our own strength. Grace counteracts fear because even if there is failure or relapse, forgiveness is available. Thus, one gets back up immediately and continues the pilgrimage of discovery.

REFLECTIONS

_____

_____

_____

_____

_____

_____

The only people who achieve much are those who want knowledge so badly that they seek it while conditions are still unfavorable. Favorable conditions never come.

— C. S. Lewis

MAY 31

Then Satan entered into Judas called Iscariot, who was one of the twelve. He went away and conferred with the chief priests and officers how he might betray him to them.

Luke 22:3-4

DARK POWERS

There have been times when I have believed that dark powers were at work in a particular person's life, bringing pain and heartache. We know very few details of Judas Iscariot's life. Although Judas was the human means of resistance at the Last Supper, Scripture makes it clear that another dimension of the resistance was demonic. Even so, Jesus did not interrupt His mission, and God's will ultimately prevailed. We often forget that the devil is God's devil! Our challenge then is not to focus on the evil one, but instead, on God's love.

REFLECTIONS

_____

_____

_____

_____

_____

_____

At the heart of the story stands the cross of Christ where evil did its worst and met its match.

—John W. Wenham

JUNE

Perhaps, indeed, the better the gift we pray for, the more time is necessary for its arrival. To give us the spiritual gift we desire, God may have to begin far back in our spirit, in regions unknown to us, and do much work that we can be aware of only in the results....

— George MacDonald

JUNE 1

God resists the proud, but gives grace to the humble. Therefore humble yourselves under the mighty hand of God, that he might exalt you in due time.

1 Peter 5:5-6

CELEBRATING EVERY DAY THINGS

When we lack humility we may begin to worship the extraordinary and have disdain for everyday life, the ordinary, small, or mundane. We cry out for the big time. The preacher wants huge crowds; the business person wants to strike it rich; the professor rushes to publish more papers. We want more media coverage, a larger office in a better location, extraordinary accomplishment in our chosen field. We come to hate our ordinary marriage, our ordinary home, our ordinary looks, our ordinary lives. We hate the thought of being average — although the very meaning of the word ensures that most of us are average. With God's love, the ordinary become the extraordinary...the pathway to glory.

REFLECTIONS

We meet no ordinary people in our lives.
— C.S. Lewis

And he said to them, "Take care, and be on your guard against all covetousness, for one's life does not consist in the abundance of his possessions."

Luke 12:15

THE INVISIBLE ESSENTIALS

The Christian faces two major realities – the physical and spiritual. Our faith calls us to accept the spiritual as a predominant reality and the physical symbolic of it. A meal is not just satisfying a biological craving but a witness of God's spiritual provision for us. The invisible essentials – love, faith, joy, peace, truth, kindness – need to take precedence over the material world in which we live.

REFLECTIONS

We are not rich by what we possess but by what we can do without.
— Immanuel Kant

Then he poured water into a basin and began to wash the disciples' feet and to wipe them with the towel that was wrapped around him.

John 13:5

TOWEL AND BASIN SIMPLICITY

Jesus lived with an inner harmony of heart that translated into outward harmony, pure and striking simplicity. After taking off his outer garments and wrapping himself in a towel, our Lord used a basin of water and a towel to wash the disciples' feet. We see Jesus using the simple objects – water, a basin, and a towel – to express his love and commitment to his disciples. Too often we make relationships so complex we ignore the simple, the ordinary.

REFLECTIONS

_____

_____

_____

_____

_____

_____

Simple can be harder than complex: You have to work hard to get your thinking clean to make it simple. But it's worth it in the end because once you get there, you can move mountains.

— Steve Jobs

JUNE 4

*One pretends to be rich, yet has nothing; another pretends to be poor,
yet has great wealth.*

Proverbs 13:7

DUPLICITY IS BONDAGE

Humble hearts recognize that there is more to life than
who ends up with the most toys. Simplicity is freedom;
duplicity is bondage. Simplicity brings joy and balance;
duplicity brings anxiety and fear. Simple things: the
commitment to keep your promises, live within your means
emotionally and financially and always consider the interest of
others ahead of your own. These are the building blocks of
character and peace of mind that are within reach for every
individual.

REFLECTIONS

---

*A man may lose the good things of this life against his will; but if he loses
the eternal blessings, he does so with his own consent.*

— St. Augustine

JUNE 5

Let what you say be simply 'Yes' or 'No'; anything more than this comes from evil.

Matthew 5:37

SAY WHAT YOU MEAN

So often we ramble on and on, cluttering our conversations with unnecessary words and complicated jargon. Being direct and concise aids communication and leaves more time for listening. The Sermon on the Mount can be regarded as Jesus' instruction book on how to live in God's kingdom while here on the earth.

My natural tendency is to speak, even to be verbose. But I have come to realize that my words should be fewer and I should give myself time to listen. Then when I talk, I can speak from the heart, the integrated part of my life, rather than just from my mind.

REFLECTIONS

_____

_____

_____

_____

_____

_____

For I have promises to keep and miles to go before I sleep.

— Robert Frost

JUNE 6

If anyone would come after me, let him deny himself and take up his cross and follow me.

Matthew 16:24

ETHICAL NARCISSISM

The first level of moral development is ethical narcissism. According to Lawrence Kohlberg, one of my mentors at Harvard, the earliest and most infantile form of moral reasoning is ethical narcissism or, in the vernacular, "all for me baby. I'm going to take care of me. Numero Uno. It's a matter of survival of the fittest."

In this immature stage we have no interest in serving others – unless, of course, it brings benefit to us. In the story of the Good Samaritan, the "good" religious men who walked by the beaten and wounded man are examples of this ethical narcissism.

REFLECTIONS

_____

_____

_____

_____

_____

_____

The most sublime act is to set another before you.

— William Blake

And he told them a parable, saying, "The land of a rich man produced plentifully, and he thought to himself, 'What shall I do, for I have nowhere to store my crops?' And he said, 'I will do this: I will tear down my barns and build larger ones, and there I will store all my grain and my goods. And I will say to my soul, "Soul, you have ample goods laid up for many years; relax, eat, drink, be merry."' But God said to him, 'Fool! This night your soul is required of you, and the things you have prepared, whose will they be?' So is the one who lays up treasure for himself and is not rich toward God.

Luke 12:16-21

ETHICAL HEDONISM

The second level of moral development is ethical hedonism: "Life is a mess, but get what you can get out of it. Eat, drink, and be merry for tomorrow we may die." This "grab-the-gusto" ethic leaves little room for service because we are too busy gratifying our own desires to meet the needs of others.

REFLECTIONS

_____

_____

_____

_____

_____

_____

All men who live only according to their five senses, and seek nothing beyond the gratification of their natural appetites for pleasure and reputation and power, cut themselves off from that charity which is the principle of all spiritual vitality and happiness because it alone saves us from the barren wilderness of our own abominable selfishness.

— Thomas Merton

JUNE 8

Which of these three, do you think, proved to be a neighbor to the man who fell among the robbers?" He said, "The one who showed him mercy." And Jesus said to him, "You go, and do likewise".

Luke 10:36-37

ETHICAL RELATIVISM

After being asked how one attains eternal life, our Lord replied, "Love God and love your neighbor as yourself." The young man tries to justify himself by asking, "Who is my neighbor?" Jesus tells him the parable of the Good Samaritan which illustrates the third level of moral development, ethical relativism. In this level of moral development, we are encouraged to "Take care of our own. Help our family, our group, our race and forget the rest." This mindset allows for limited service to those who prequalify, but leads to selfish exploitation or oppression of one group by another, which overrides brotherly compassion. The Good Samaritan went beyond the relativism of race and religion, to care for the wounded man.

REFLECTIONS

_____

_____

_____

_____

_____

_____

...Today the lack of faith is an expression of profound confusion and despair. Once skepticism and rationalism were progressive forces for the development of thought; now they have become rationalizations for relativism and uncertainty.

— Erich Fromm

JUNE 9

No one can serve two masters, for either he will hate the one and love the other, or he will be devoted to the one and despise the other. You cannot serve God and money.

Matthew 6:24

ETHICAL AUTHORITARIANISM

The fourth stage of moral development is ethical authoritarianism. This flawed reasoning says, "Yes sir, I know it was wrong, but I was just following orders." This was the Nuremburg defense used by Nazis to excuse their evil treatment of Jews. Anything or anyone we give unquestioned obedience to without examining our moral reasoning, can be destructive. At this level we may recognize our responsibility to serve our fellow man but we rationalize our way out of it with noble sounding excuses.

REFLECTIONS

_____

_____

_____

_____

_____

_____

The development of science and of the creative activities of the spirit requires a freedom that consists in the independence of thought from the restrictions of authoritarian and social prejudice.

— Albert Einstein

JUNE 10

If you pay attention to the one who wears the fine clothing and say, "You sit here in a good place," while you say to the poor man, "You stand over there," or "Sit down at my feet" have you not then made distinctions among yourselves and become judges with evil thoughts?

James 2:3-4

ETHICAL UTILITARIANISM

The fifth level of moral development is ethical utilitarianism, the greatest good for the greatest number or the most powerful. This works well for you if you're included in the greatest number, part of the "in" group. But in such a philosophy, no one is really safe because standards may shift, making us no longer one of the privileged. Christ's teaching of providing service for the least among us is not part of this plan.

REFLECTIONS

_____

_____

_____

_____

_____

_____

When a poor person dies of hunger it has not happened because God did not take care of him or her. It has happened because neither you nor I wanted to give that person what he or she needed.

— Mother Teresa

JUNE 11

When he had washed their feet and put on his outer garments and resumed his place, he said to them, "Do you understand what I have done to you? You call me Teacher and Lord, and you are right, for so I am. If I then, your Lord and Teacher, have washed your feet, you also ought to wash one another's feet".

John 13:12-14

THE MEANING OF COMMUNITY

Over the last four days, I have presented five stages of moral development. The truth is that none of these flawed ethics work. My conviction is we need an ethic that brings about the meaning of community and personal values of service to our families, neighbors, and world. This ethic is reflected in Christ washing his disciples' feet and his well-known parable of the Good Samaritan. Our calling in Christ is to serve in love.

REFLECTIONS

_____

_____

_____

_____

_____

_____

Everybody can be great...because anybody can serve. You don't have to have a college degree to serve. You don't have to make your subject and verb agree to serve. You only need a heart full of grace. A soul generated by love.

— Martin Luther King, Jr.

JUNE 12

Therefore, if anyone is in Christ, he is a new creation. The old has passed away; behold, the new has come.

2 Corinthians 5:17

NEW BEGINNINGS

When we choose to commit our lives to Christ and receive his forgiveness, we are re-created and his spirit comes to live within us. We are made new in Christ; our bodies become the sanctuary of the Holy God. This is the mystery Paul spoke of when he wrote, "Christ in you, the hope of glory."

REFLECTIONS

_____

_____

_____

_____

_____

_____

True education is a kind of never ending story — a matter of continual beginnings, of habitual fresh starts, of persistent newness.

— J.R.R. Tolkien

But a Samaritan, as he journeyed, came to where he was, and when he saw him, he had compassion. He went to him and bound up his wounds, pouring on oil and wine. Then he set him on his own animal and brought him to an inn and took care of him. And the next day he took out two denarii and gave them to the innkeeper, saying, 'Take care of him, and whatever more you spend, I will repay you when I come back.'

Luke 10:33-35

THE UNVEILED HEART

Jesus knew from experience that the way of the earth is hard, fraught with struggle, tears, and tragedy. And those who would grasp the meaning of life must be willing to listen to the pain, soothe the hurt, and wash the feet of fellow travelers. Jesus had shown the disciples what He meant by serving one another in the parable of the Good Samaritan. The Samaritan saw the wounded man and had compassion on him. The unveiled heart identifies with others and empathizes with their pain.

REFLECTIONS

_____

_____

_____

_____

_____

_____

It is easy enough to be friendly to one's friends. But to befriend the one who regards himself as your enemy is the quintessence of true religion. The other is mere business.

— Mahatma Gandhi

JUNE 14

If I speak in the tongues of men and of angels, but have not love, I am a noisy gong or a clanging cymbal. And if I have prophetic powers, and understand all mysteries and all knowledge, and if I have all faith, so as to remove mountains, but have not love, I am nothing. If I give away all I have, and if I deliver up my body to be burned, but have not love, I gain nothing.

1 Corinthians 13:1-7

AND HAVE NOT LOVE

The apostle Paul warns that although we give the ultimate service ("Giving our bodies to be burned") if we do not serve from the heart ("Have not love"), it is useless. How paradoxical! Surely if someone sacrifices his or her body, it must be considered good. Not so! God, the final Evaluator of the seen and unseen, judges us by the motivation of the heart.

REFLECTIONS

_____

_____

_____

_____

_____

_____

It is in giving that we receive.

— St. Francis of Assisi

JUNE 15

...whoever wishes to be first among you shall be slave of all. For even the Son of Man did not come to be served, but to serve, and to give His life a ransom for many.

Mark 10:44-45

SERVICE TO OTHERS

Spiritually mature worship means being committed to the service of others. It is often easier to serve ourselves, but at the Last Supper Christ taught the true meaning and fulfillment in life, and into eternity, allows the love of God to be expressed through us in service to others. It is a willing service, rushing forth from the heart overflowing with love and centered in Christ, not a compulsive or obligatory set of actions clothed in drudgery.

REFLECTIONS

_____

_____

_____

_____

_____

_____

The service you do for others is the rent you pay for your room here on earth.

—Muhammad Ali

Peter said to him, "You shall never wash my feet." Jesus answered him, "If I do not wash you, you have no share with me."

John 13:8

SERVANT LEADERSHIP

With the towel and basin of water, Christ proceeded to wash his disciples' feet. Peter represented each of us when he asked a question of incredulity, "Lord, are you washing *my* feet?" The answer was obvious; Jesus had already washed other disciples' feet. Peter was disturbed by the role his leader chose to play. In his mind he just could not see a man of authority taking the role of a servant. Could he follow a leader who is willing to stoop so low?

REFLECTIONS

_____

_____

_____

_____

_____

_____

If you would convince a man that he does wrong, do right. But do not care to convince him. Men will believe what they see. Let them see.

— Henry David Thoreau

JUNE 17

Give thanks in all circumstances; for this is the will of God in Christ Jesus for you.

1 Thessalonians 5:18

APPRECIATION

Christ gave Peter the option of allowing him to wash his feet like a servant or to have no part in the work of the kingdom. In effect he was saying, "If you want to belong, you have to be willing to receive what I have to give." A lot of us, particularly men, can give, but we find it very hard to receive. We find it even more difficult to say, "Thank you," or "I appreciate you." Christ is saying that when we discover our potential in life, we will realize that it is not only important to give, but also to receive.

Imagine what would happen today if we turn to our boss, our wife, or even our children and said, "I really appreciate you. Thank you for your help."

REFLECTIONS

_____

_____

_____

_____

_____

_____

Appreciation is a wonderful thing. It makes what is excellent in others belong to us as well.

— Voltaire

And your ancient ruins shall be rebuilt; you shall raise up the foundations of many generations; you shall be called the repairer of the breach, the restorer of streets to dwell in.

Isaiah 58:12

WOUNDED HEALERS

A grateful heart qualifies us to become healers, repairers of the breach, and builders of broken walls. Only when we are vulnerable to receive can we truly give. Church leaders, pastors, and lay people often want to be seen as examples of the victorious life, as people who "have it all together." Instead could it be that the Lord is calling us to be "wounded healers," admitting our pain and being willing to receive help? Are we willing to admit our needs or to receive correction even from those who are in our care?

REFLECTIONS

_____

_____

_____

_____

_____

_____

Ring the bells that still can ring.
Forget the perfect offering.
There's a crack in everything;
That's how the light gets in.
— Leonard Cohen. *Anthem*

JUNE 19

And as he entered a village, he was met by ten lepers, who stood at a distance and lifted up their voices, saying, "Jesus, Master, have mercy on us." When he saw them he said to them, "Go and show yourselves to the priests." And as they went they were cleansed. Then one of them, when he saw that he was healed, turned back, praising God with a loud voice; and he fell on his face at Jesus' feet, giving him thanks. Now he was a Samaritan. Then Jesus answered, "Were not ten cleansed? Where are the nine? Was no one found to return and give praise to God except this foreigner?"

Luke 17:12-18

WHERE ARE THE NINE?

During our Lord's mission on earth he healed many people. In one incident, he healed ten lepers, but only one of the lepers returned to thank him. Christ asked, "Where are the other nine?" This question was a powerful statement that implied the other nine are missing something. Their healing was incomplete. Gratitude is a reflection of an open, overflowing heart. The cure of the leprosy was a powerful miracle, but the opening of the closed heart to faith and gratitude is the quintessential meaning of life.

REFLECTIONS

_____

_____

_____

_____

_____

_____

Piglet noticed that even though he had a Very Small Heart, it could hold a rather large amount of Gratitude.

— A.A. Milne, *Winnie-the-Pooh*

JUNE 20

For I consider that the sufferings of this present time are not worth comparing with the glory that is to be revealed in us.

Romans 8:18

JOY IN SUFFERING

Finding fulfillment in the midst of rejection or pain is the gift of God. It is this joy that the angels sang to the shepherds when the baby Jesus was born. In coming full circle at the end of His life, it was because of the anticipated joy of our salvation that Christ endured the cross. Joy and fulfillment are not experienced apart from pain but beyond it. Like Jesus, we will find that the completion of our inner fulfillment comes independently of the visible results or the response of others to our work.

REFLECTIONS

_____

_____

_____

_____

_____

_____

Suffering has been stronger than all other teaching, and has taught me to understand what your heart used to be. I have been bent and broken, but - I hope - into a better shape.

— Charles Dickens

"Whoever receives you receives me, and whoever receives me receives him who sent me.... And whoever gives one of these little ones even a cup of cold water because he is a disciple, truly, I say to you, he will by no means lose his reward."

Matthew 10:40a, 42

INHERITED INCARNATION

Jesus reveals to his disciple that when they go out in his name, they are his incarnational presence. Those who honor them, honor him. Those who give them a cup of cold water, refresh the Lord himself. This had to be a deeply humbling moment. He was not saying that they were to be worshiped as God nor were they to see this as an authoritarian position. In a unique way the incarnation of God in human form happened only once – when "the Word became flesh and dwelt among us," but in another sense the incarnation continues as Christ is embodied in our lives.

REFLECTIONS

_____

_____

_____

_____

_____

_____

There is nothing so secular that it cannot be sacred, and that is one of the deepest messages of the Incarnation.

— Madeleine L'Engle

JUNE 22

He himself bore our sins in his body on the tree, that we might die to sin and live to righteousness. By his wounds you have been healed.

1 Peter 2:24

LIFE IS WOUNDED

Life is wounded! In order to liberate ourselves, we have to work through our hurt trails to be open to our love story. Committing to love simply means opening to the experience of God's presence in our lives and recognizing that the presence is manifested by his loving care, which spreads between us as well as throughout nature.

REFLECTIONS

_____

_____

_____

_____

_____

_____

The world without is desolate... Except for the world within.

— Wallace Stevens

I baptize you with water for repentance, but he who is coming after me is mightier than I, whose sandals I am not worthy to carry. He will baptize you with the Holy Spirit and fire.

Matthew 3:11

THE FIRE OF GOD'S BURNING LOVE

Contemplation is a deep form of spirituality in which we commit to the intention of allowing God's presence in our lives. Going against the grain of our modern society, with all its hustle and bustle, contemplative spirituality calls us to the importance of silence in waiting for the guidance of God through the Holy Spirit. The focus here is on being, rather than doing. This does not mean that in contemplative spirituality, we are lazy and refuse to do. Instead, it means that the fire of God's burning love in our hearts is manifested by showing love and caring for those around us.

REFLECTIONS

_____

_____

_____

_____

_____

_____

The intimacy of a house of love always leads to a solidarity with the weak, the closer we come to the heart of the One who loves us with an unconditional love, the closer we come to each other and the solidarity of a redeemed humanity.

— Henri Nouwen

JUNE 24

The purpose in a man's heart is like deep water, but an understanding man will draw it out.

Proverbs 20:5

THE MEANING OF THE HEART

What is the heart? Obviously I do not mean the physical organ, but since medieval times the heart has been a metaphor for the center of our being. It is the place where love and hate coexist. It is the decision making center where all our choices – good and evil – are decided. It is the part of ourselves where we relate to the beautiful and the ugly, the holy and the profane. The heart is both conscious and unconscious. In a sense the heart is the universe within – as wide as the heavens above. But more than anything, the heart is the place where we meet God.

REFLECTIONS

_____

_____

_____

_____

_____

_____

Therefore he willed that the hearts of Men should seek beyond the world and should find no rest therein; but they should have a virtue to shape their life, amid the powers and chances of the world.

— J.R.R. Tolkien

Keep your heart with all vigilance, for from it flow the springs of life.
Proverbs 4:23

INTIMACY AND SPIRITUALITY

In essence intimacy and spirituality are really all about the heart. The Bible warns us to guard our heart because out of that flows the issues of our life. This is an ancient saying but so hard for us to absorb. The reality is that most of our issues come from within us, and it takes a lot of courage to realize that persons or situations outside our control do not cause them. But this is also very hopeful, because the only person we can work with or change is our self. In essence, the issues of spirituality and intimacy are very personal and everyone has to make their own decisions.

REFLECTIONS

_____

_____

_____

_____

_____

_____

Not hero worship, but intimacy with Christ.
— Dietrich Bonhoeffer

JUNE 26

His left hand is under my head, and his right hand embraces me!
Song of Solomon 2:6

THE CHALLENGE OF INTIMACY

The challenge of intimacy, like the challenge of contemplation, is to make the journey to our hearts, to the place where we truly exist. In essence contemplation and intimacy mean living from the heart. But this is not as easy as it seems. As a Bahamian saying goes, "I've been to Nassau, I've been to Abaco, I've been to Harbor Island, but I've never been to me." Tragically many of us live and die without experiencing more the depth of our hearts. God waits in our heart, whether we are aware of it or not, inviting us to commune with him. We ignore this invitation at our peril!

REFLECTIONS

_____

_____

_____

_____

_____

_____

Contemplation is the highest expression of man's intellectual and spiritual life. It is that life itself fully awake, fully active, fully aware that it is alive... It is spontaneous awe at the sacredness of life, of being.
— Thomas Merton

JUNE 27

As the Father has loved me, so have I loved you. Abide in my love.

John 15:9

A LIFE OF LOVE

Expressing the deepest form of love, Jesus said to his disciples, "As the Father has loved me, so have I loved you" (John 15:9). Contemplation and intimacy emanate from love, and our Lord reminds us that his love reaches out to us in the most despairing and difficult points of our lives. This is especially meaningful because it challenges us to live a life of love.

REFLECTIONS

_____

_____

_____

_____

_____

_____

The opposite of Loneliness is not Togetherness , It's Intimacy.

— Richard Bach

JUNE 28

Blessed be God, because he has not rejected my prayer or removed his steadfast love from me!

Psalm 66:20

ACCEPTING GOD'S LOVE

Regardless of how much we may have failed, how fallen we have become, or how much we feel like outcasts, Jesus reminds us that we are loved. Contemplation is opening ourselves to the deep love of God, which restores the meaning of our identity. Contemplation is the experience of living from the heart, of accepting that God loves us as we are...and not as we should be!

REFLECTIONS

_____

_____

_____

_____

_____

_____

Don't waste yourself in rejection, nor bark against the bad, but chant the beauty of the good.

— Ralph Waldo Emerson

June 29

Surely goodness and love will follow me all the days of my life, and I will dwell in the house of the Lord forever.

—Psalm 23:6

The Sunshine of God's Love

Intimacy involves opening up to the love of God while contemplation involves coming to a deep and liberating realization that our identity, above all else, is based on being the beloved of God. Basking in the warm sunshine of God's love, we move beyond our inauthentic selves to our true selves as the beloved of God. Our small "I" is followed up by the great "I Am" and as a result we live in God and he lives in us.

Reflections

_____

_____

_____

_____

_____

_____

The Christian does not think God will love us because we are good, but that God will make us good because He loves us.

— C.S. Lewis

June 30

Blessed are those who mourn, for they will be comforted.

Matthew 5:4

The Hurt Trail

Many of us have within ourselves a powerful hurt trail involving aspects of abandonment, rejection, humiliation, guilt, and shame. As a result it is very easy to allow our hearts to become filled with all the anger and hurt in our lives, leaving no space for love. As we open our lives to working on ourselves in therapy or deep prayer, we empty ourselves of hurt and anger, creating in our hearts a loving place where we can be at one with God, each other, and ourselves.

Reflections

_____

_____

_____

_____

_____

_____

The root of Christian love is not the will to love but the faith that one is loved.

—Thomas Merton

July

Over the years we have developed the idea that being present to people in all their needs is our greatest and primary vocation. The Bible does not seem to support this. Jesus' primary concern was to be obedient to his Father, to live constantly in his presence. Only then did it become clear to him what his task was in his relationships with people.

— Henri Nouwen

July 1

Be still, and know that I am God.

Psalm 46:10

A Trinity of Communion

The spiritual journey at its heart is really all about a trinity of communion: communion with God, ourselves and others. The essence of the gospel is that God loves us and is always seeking communion with us. We cannot have sweet communion with the love who seeks us without being vulnerable and in communion with others. Also, we cannot allow ourselves to be cut off from communion with our own deepest self, our heart. Oh Lord, help us to open up to your love.

Reflections

_____

_____

_____

_____

_____

_____

It is, I think, that we are all so alone in what lies deepest in our souls, so unable to find the words, and perhaps the courage to speak with unlocked hearts, that we don't know at all that it is the same with others
— Sheldon Vanauken, *A Severe Mercy*

July 2

You prepare a table before me in the presence of my enemies.

Psalm 23:5

The Silence of Communion with God

Communion with God always involves silence. Opening ourselves to external silence creates interior silence and interior silence creates stillness, making space for God and ourselves to sit at the table set for two. Experiencing the presence of God in silence is a discipline, a learning experience. In the silence of contemplation we open ourselves to the naked love of God's presence, which bathes our souls, creating the deepest form of intimacy and communion.

Reflections

_____

_____

_____

_____

_____

_____

The man who fears to be alone will never be anything but lonely, no matter how much he may surround himself with people.

— Thomas Merton

Whoever is slow to anger has great understanding, but he who has a hasty temper exalts folly.

Proverbs 14:29

OUR OWN WORST ENEMY

Hurt and anger in our hearts make us our own worst enemy and, as a result, we become experts at self-sabotage. Repressed anger causes resentment. Resentment (re-sentiment) means feeling over and over again our hurts from the past which in turn creates anger. The hurt and anger build up and create resistance in our hearts and make it difficult to experience the love of God, others, and self.

REFLECTIONS

_____

_____

_____

_____

_____

_____

Anybody can become angry — that is easy, but to be angry with the right person and to the right degree and at the right time and for the right purpose, and in the right way — that is not within everybody's power and is not easy.

— Aristotle

*A hot-tempered man stirs up strife, but he who is slow to **anger** quiets contention.*

Proverbs 15:18

RESISTANCE

Resistance in our spiritual journey is usually associated with, if not caused by, anger. Much anger results from the effect of our repressed childhood trauma presenting itself in our adult lives. It may, of course, be provoked, but a person can only provoke the anger that is already in our hearts. Painful as it may seem, anger is a message from the heart to come home to ourselves. By facing and working through the hurt and anger in our hearts, we open ourselves to the deep love of God. Through a ripple effect this creates intimacy in the distant world around us.

REFLECTIONS

He has great tranquility of heart who cares neither for the praises nor the fault-finding of men. He will easily be content and pacified, whose conscience is pure.

— Thomas à Kempis

July 5

He leads the humble in what is right, and teaches the humble his way.
Psalm 25:9

A Foundation of Humility

Humility is the foundation block of spirituality and contemplation. It always leads to intimacy. In essence, humility is facing the truth about our lives: learning to accept ourselves as we are — not as we would like to be or feel we should be. Taking off his outer garment, our Lord took upon himself the garb of a slave to give himself in service to his disciples and wash their feet. As we open to God's love we have to be willing to allow God to expose our prejudices, our superior attitudes, our competitive jealousies and our alienating tendencies. We then have to be willing to let go of them.

Reflections

_____

_____

_____

_____

_____

_____

If you can't explain it to a six year old, you don't understand it yourself.
— Albert Einstein

JULY 6

Those that were sown on the good soil are the ones who hear the word and accept it and bear fruit, thirtyfold and sixtyfold and a hundredfold.

Mark 4:19-20

GOOD GROUND

Humility has its derivation from the Latin word 'humus' which means soil. Humility involves preparing the soil of our hearts to grow the seeds of God's love in our lives. I believe many of us have allowed our hearts to harden and it is difficult for the seeds of love to grow. This unplowed ground must be tilled by working through the very painful hurts and experiences of anger that so often characterize our deep inner selves. As we open our hearts to the presence of God in our lives, he creates fertile ground where the seed of love can prosper.

REFLECTIONS

_____

_____

_____

_____

_____

There is nothing noble in being superior to your fellow man; true nobility is being superior to your former self.

— Ernest Hemingway

JULY 7

*Remember the word that I said to you: 'A **servant** is not greater than his master.' If they persecuted me, they will also persecute you. If they kept my word, they will also keep yours.*

John 15:20

THE SERVANT GOD

Dressed as a slave, our Lord bowed and washed his disciples' feet. What a paradox, the holy almighty God washing the feet of ordinary, lowly human beings. This and this alone is God's love, providing a beautiful picture of contemplation and intimacy. Though the Lord God is high and mighty, his love is always towards those who are humble and contrite. This foot washing demonstrates the love which never fails us, a love which reminds us that Christ still washes our feet by sending us friends to encourage us, children to admire us, and spouses to love us.

REFLECTIONS

A great man is always willing to be little.
— Ralph Waldo Emerson

JULY 8

Create in me a clean heart, O God, and renew a right spirit within me.

Psalm 51:10

CLEANSING THANKFULNESS

Contemplation means not just the giving of love but also deep appreciation of receiving love. It involves saying sincerely from the heart, "thank you" or "I appreciate you." What a revolution might occur if we learned to express our gratitude and appreciation more freely to our children, spouses and those who work with us. Thankfulness has a way of cleansing the air and creating a loving open community.

REFLECTIONS

_____

_____

_____

_____

_____

_____

Let us be grateful to the people who make us happy; they are the charming gardeners who make our souls blossom.

— Marcel Proust

JULY 9

We are afflicted in every way, but not crushed; perplexed, but not driven to despair.

2 Corinthians 4:8

TRIANGLE OF DESPAIR

Our false self forms onion-like layers around our heart, creating the triangle of abandonment, rejection, and humiliation. This is so intractable that our hearts become like stone and even though love may be close to us, staring us in the face, it is very difficult to open our hearts to receive it. We don't have to live this way and destroy ourselves; we can stop and change. I believe Jesus washed Judas' feet the most carefully of all. This is a very powerful lesson. Love is not just getting along with those who appreciate us, but in a very deep sense means moving in love even towards those who would use us or reject us.

REFLECTIONS

When I despair, I remember that all through history the way of truth and love have always won. There have been tyrants and murderers, and for a time, they can seem invincible, but in the end, they always fall. Think of it--always.

— Mahatma Gandhi

JULY 10

As Jesus said, "Now that I, your Lord and Teacher, have washed your feet, you also should wash one another's feet."

John 13:14

TENDER LOVING CARE

Today, many of us are tired, working extremely hard, and stressed with many pressures. We need to have our feet washed, but it is important to wash each other's feet. This may be literally or figuratively– a kind word, an encouraging hug, a letter or phone call.

REFLECTIONS

_____

_____

_____

_____

_____

_____

How far you go in life depends on your being tender with the young, compassionate with the aged, sympathetic with the striving and tolerant of the weak and strong. Because someday in your life you will have been all of these.

— George Washington Carver

JULY 11

And I, when I am lifted up from the earth, will draw all people to myself.
John 12:32

THE VERTICAL AND HORIZONTAL LIFE

There is a vital connection between the vertical concept of worship and holiness, and the horizontal concept of the glory of God reflected in the beauty in the earth. Life without worship leaves us soulless and ungrateful. We begin to feel we deserve everything and develop the illusion that everything we earn is ours. We forget that life itself is a grace; even the air we breathe is a gift. Our hearts become hardened, making us angry, ungrateful, possessive...and lonely.

REFLECTIONS

_____

_____

_____

_____

_____

_____

The same forces that have destroyed the mystery of holiness, have destroyed the mystery of beauty.

— Herbert Read

July 12

Humble yourselves, therefore, under the mighty hand of God so that at the proper time he may exalt you.

1 Peter 5:6

Shattered Dreams

By the age of 45 or 50, many of us have confronted shattered dreams and live with the painful reality of what might have been. We can choose to live the rest of our lives in a state of anger and frustration or we can recognize our failures and losses, grieve our pain, and open ourselves to a lifestyle of faithfulness and gratitude. In order to understand the deeper parts of our heart, to experience the love of our true selves in God, we must choose to deal with the angry feelings in our hearts. Otherwise they will contaminate every other area of our lives, and impede contemplation. In contemplation we experience the reformation of emotions. As a result, anger, instead of being a threat, becomes a positive motivating force to fight injustice and other wrongs of the world.

Reflections

_____

_____

_____

_____

_____

_____

Beyond the picket fences and the oil wells, the happy endings, and the fairy tales, is the reality of shattered lives and broken dreams. We carry on.

— Tim McGraw

July 13

He who is in you is greater than he [the evil one] who is in the world.

1 John 4:4

The armor of god

Because the battle is spiritual, the weapons of our warfare must also be spiritual. We are told in Ephesians 6:10-18 to put on the full armor of God:

The sword of the Spirit (the Word of God)

The breast plate of righteousness (obedience to Christ)

The helmet of salvation (the sure knowledge of God's saving love)

The shoes of the good news of peace (the forgiveness and reconciliation we have received because of Christ's death in our place)

Reliance on these great spiritual truths must be buttressed by continual prayer as we constantly look to God's strength rather than our own.

Reflections

_____

_____

_____

_____

_____

_____

All human nature vigorously resists grace because grace changes us and the change is painful.

— Flannery O'Connor

July 14

I feared the people [more than I feared God] and obeyed their voice.
1 Samuel 15: 24

CONFORMITY

Perhaps the most powerful external resistance to growth is the power of the social environment. King Saul, when asked why he had refused to obey God's command to destroy the Amalekites, replied that he feared the people more than God.

Conformity is so powerful that many of us throw away our best efforts in order to please the crowd or gain social acceptance. People develop a fear of rejection by the surrounding society. Yet the crowd is fickle. After all, the crowd called for the crucifixion of Jesus.

The goal cannot be to win acceptance from others but rather to live true to our convictions and to our God.

REFLECTIONS

_____

_____

_____

_____

_____

_____

To be one's self, and unafraid whether right or wrong, is more admirable than the easy cowardice of surrender to conformity.

— Irving Wallace

JULY 15

Put off your old self, which belongs to your former manner of life and is corrupt through deceitful desires, and be renewed in the spirit of your minds.

Ephesians 4:22-23

SAY GOODBYE TO THE OLD

Secure persons will encourage growth in another, while less secure friends or relatives become threatened, withdrawn and critical. The road to discovery involves saying goodbye to the security of home, the old influences, empty traditions, and harmful patterns of family relationships. Only if we are willing to say goodbye to the old can we say hello to the new community of persons who choose to transcend the daily march of mediocrity and instead, reach for the stars.

REFLECTIONS

_____

_____

_____

_____

_____

_____

In that book which is my memory,
On the first page of the chapter that is the day when I first met you,
Appear the words, 'Here begins a new life'.

— Dante Alighieri, *Vita Nuova*

July 16

He who did not spare his own Son but gave him up for us all, how will he not also with him graciously give us all things?

Romans 8:32

REJECTION

Perhaps the hardest thing about moving into discovery is the realization that we may have to stand alone. Sometimes this involves the rejection of those close to us. The truth is that people fail us. Even in the church some of our closest associates will disagree or speak against us. It is natural to feel hurt and angry and want revenge when this happens. But the challenge of our faith is to firmly push on with our convictions in an attitude of love and compassion.

REFLECTIONS

_____

_____

_____

_____

_____

_____

Whatever is rejected from the self, appears in the world as an event.

— C.G. Jung

Who, though he was in the form of God, did not count equality with God a thing to be grasped, but emptied himself, by taking the form of a servant.

Philippians 2:6-7

FACING TRIALS

How we deal with mild or severe resistance will change our heart – for good or for evil. It is not only a traumatic event that works against us, but our response to the situation can be even more destructive than the actual event. In this section we will look at some ways you can face resistance and move on in your journey towards discovery.

We may want to run away. Our heart may try to hide or escape, but the resistance must be met as an unavoidable pit on the path of discovery. Trials and tribulations do not have to stop the process of spiritual growth. Rather, these unwelcomed S.T.O.R.Ms (**S**ignificant **T**rauma **O**verwhelming **R**easonable **M**inds) in life can help us clarify our values and gain a clearer view of God's love.

REFLECTIONS

_____

_____

_____

_____

_____

_____

Courage is resistance to fear, mastery of fear — not absence of fear.
— Mark Twain

JULY 18

Therefore I tell you, do not be anxious about your life, what you will eat or what you will drink, nor about your body, what you will put on. Is not life more than food, and the body more than clothing?

Matthew 6:25

TODAY IS THE DAY

One of the cruelest lies associated with the illusion that we can ignore today and procrastinate until tomorrow, is the belief that we can pass up an opportunity to express love to those we care about because there is always tomorrow. There is no illusion of permanence. Things will not always be as they are today. People die, things change and opportunities for heartfelt conversation are lost. Discovery calls us to live the truth in the present reality, making the most of the time we are allotted on earth.

REFLECTIONS

_____

_____

_____

_____

_____

_____

Worry does not empty tomorrow of its sorrow, it empties today of its strength.

— Corrie ten Boom

Judge not, that you be not judged. For with the judgment you pronounce you will be judged, and with the measure you use it will be measured to you.

Matthew 7:1-2

CHERISHED NOTIONS

Communion is difficult because in connecting with others we must give up some of our cherished notions, preconceived ideas, prejudices, and old ways of looking at things. We cannot always be right. Because we are uncomfortable with the strong emotions that often accompany intimacy, we may develop a lifestyle that leaves little room for genuine fellowship. We must resist the tendency to alienate ourselves from everyone, making it impossible to enjoy love, warmth and intimacy.

REFLECTIONS

_____

_____

_____

_____

_____

_____

If you judge people, you have no time to love them.

— Mother Teresa

JULY 20

Let not sin therefore reign in your mortal body, to make you obey its passions.

Romans 6:12

EMOTIONAL BUTTONS

Family members know about our emotional buttons and they're very effective in pushing them at the wrong time. We are more vulnerable to the comments of those who are near and dear to us. As one insightful college student remarked, "The time to tell my father about a problem is after I've successfully solved it!"

REFLECTIONS

If we find ourselves with a desire that nothing in this world can satisfy, the most probable explanation is that we were made for another world.

— C.S. Lewis

July 21

Bear one another's burdens, and so fulfill the law of Christ.

Galatians 6:2

Sharing Burdens

We need to share our burdens with one another. After the tragic death of my brother's daughter, it was important for my brother and me to talk to one another, and not allow our pain to wall us off. We may all feel the urge to withdraw from time to time, but it is important that we do not isolate ourselves in the face of resistance. There really is strength in numbers.

Even when we can't understand, we know God is still on His throne. When we can't put our feelings into words, we can take comfort in knowing God hears the groans of those who love Him.

Reflections

I carry your heart (I carry it in my heart).

— e.e. cummings

JULY 22

For everything there is a season, and a time for every matter under heaven.

Ecclesiastes 3:1

GOD'S TIMETABLE

God may operate on a different timetable from the one we prefer, but He makes all things work for good in His time. Do not be surprised by difficult trials that enter your life. Yield them to God just as simply as you do the joys and blessings. We do not have to invite harm or add to our sufferings in our effort to be spiritual. However, we should be well rooted in God's love before the inevitable storms of life hit home.

REFLECTIONS

_____

_____

_____

_____

_____

_____

All we have to decide is what to do with the time that is given us.
— J.R.R. Tolkien

Peter said to him, "You shall never wash my feet." Jesus answered him, "If I do not wash you, you have no share with me."

John 13:8

THE VULNERABLE GOD

There is no servant at the Last Supper. Christ chose that role for himself. Stripping himself of his garments, He clothed himself in the garb of a servant. By doing so he chose to divest himself of power, making a statement to His followers concerning their arrogant strivings. In essence, He was telling them, "In order to know who I am, you must learn to humble yourselves."

Many of us know the value of true humility, but we are afraid to be humble because humility requires us to be vulnerable and open.

REFLECTIONS

_____

_____

_____

_____

_____

_____

When we were children, we used to think that when we were grown-up we would no longer be vulnerable. But to grow up is to accept vulnerability.... To be alive is to be vulnerable.

— Madeleine L'Engle

JULY 24

Blessed are the meek, for they shall inherit the earth.
Matthew 5:5

GROUNDED IN HUMILITY

Humility is one of the deepest spiritual values that is borne out of our faithfulness and commitment to living a life of prayer. However, as we decide to grow in humility, we become more open to the deep hurts of shame and anger in our heart. So often, we despair and pull back. We compensate by taking on an invincible attitude. This is because we sometimes believe that humility is a sign of weakness and not strength. But in essence, humility is aligning our life with God. As a result, we don't act in our own strength but through the wisdom, power and guidance of God, who is omnipotent.

REFLECTIONS

_____

_____

_____

_____

_____

_____

Out of your vulnerabilities will come your strength.
— Sigmund Freud

To them God chose to make known how great among the Gentiles are the riches of the glory of this mystery, which is Christ in you, the hope of glory.

Colossians 1:27

CHRIST IN OTHERS

Jesus told his disciples that he was going away, but that when they received each other they were receiving him. How important it is in our spiritual journey to recognize that Jesus often comes to us in other people. Shame prevents us from recognizing the visitation of Christ in others. Only when we transcend our shame can we see Christ in the people around us. Christ is in our midst in spite of all our hurt and pain. He is the immanent reality that blesses and renews us.

REFLECTIONS

_____

_____

_____

_____

_____

_____

There is nothing like returning to a place that remains unchanged to find the ways in which you yourself have altered.

— Nelson Mandela

July 26

What if God, desiring to show his wrath and to make known his power, has endured with much patience vessels of wrath prepared for destruction?

Romans 9:22

Facing the Pseudo gods

Once we face our hearts we find much resistance to God, our deeper selves, and love in the world. Six major pseudo gods or addictions and modern culture block the heart: Narcissism, conformity, materialism, the sacredness of the affect, the bane of the extraordinary, and the illusions of permanence. Only by shattering these pseudo gods or addictions of modern culture are we able to open our hearts to experience the love that will not let us go, and the face that does not turn away.

Reflections

Once in an age God sends to some of us a friend who loves in us, not a false-imagining, an unreal character, but looking through the rubbish of our imperfections, loves in us the divine ideal of our nature,--loves, not the man that we are, but the angel that we may be.

— Harriet Beecher Stowe

JULY 27

For great is the Lord, and greatly to be praised, and he is to be feared above all gods.

1 Chronicles 16:25

GOD CENTERED

In devotional spirituality the temptation is to make ourselves the center of activity, whereas contemplative spirituality calls us to wait in silence for God and God alone. In contemplative spirituality our activity originates in God and is led by God and not by ourselves. In devotional spirituality we invite God into our heart as the guest of our life. However, in contemplative spirituality, after inviting God as a guest in our heart, we bow in humility to worship Him as the host of our life. It is all about God...and not about us. Have thine own way, Oh God!

REFLECTIONS

_____

_____

_____

_____

_____

_____

People are often unreasonable and self-centered. Forgive them anyway.
If you are kind, people may accuse you of ulterior motives. Be kind
anyway. If you are honest, people may cheat you. Be honest anyway.
If you find happiness, people may be jealous. Be happy anyway.
The good you do today may be forgotten tomorrow. Do good anyway.
Give the world the best you have and it may never be enough. Give your
best anyway. For you see, in the end, it is between you and God. It was
never between you and them anyway.

— Mother Teresa

JULY 28

Blessed are the pure in heart, for they shall see God.

Matthew 5:8

A TRANSPARENT LIFE

In contemplation, life loses its opaqueness and becomes transparent to allow us to experience the events of our life as pathways rather than obstacles to the fullness of living. Contemplation enables a growing transformation of consciousness, manifested by a life that is lived from the source of love — our true selves in God, and expressed to our fellow beings in the world around us.

REFLECTIONS

_____

_____

_____

_____

_____

_____

There is a beautiful transparency to honest disciples who never wear a false face and do not pretend to be anything but who they are.

— Brennan Manning

JULY 29

(and a sword will pierce through your own soul also), so that thoughts from many hearts may be revealed.

Luke 2:35

GRIEVING HEARTS

There is no true emptying of the heart without grieving. Drawing people together, grieving enhances intimacy. Yet because of the pain of the losses we have experienced, many of us stay at the anger pole of grief rather than working through the sadness of our grief and moving on. Full of anger, we may feel empowered but our anger prevents us from taking advantage of the love that exists around us.

REFLECTIONS

_____

_____

_____

_____

_____

_____

The world is indeed full of peril and in it there are many dark places. But still there is much that is fair. And though in all lands, love is now mingled with grief, it still grows, perhaps, the greater.

— J.R.R. Tolkien, *The Lord of the Rings*

JULY 30

And he withdrew from them about a stone's throw, and knelt down and prayed, saying, "Father, if you are willing, remove this cup from me. Nevertheless, not my will, but yours, be done".

Luke 22:41-42

LETTING GO

At the foot of the cross we must be silent because we face a mystery too deep for words. His ultimate sacrifice for our sin and shame separated Jesus from God the Father with whom he had always been one. This is the cup our Lord asked to avoid in the agony of the garden. Then, in commitment to our broken hearts and shame-based lives, he said, "Not my will, but your will be done." Healing requires that we let go of our distractions, addictions, and compulsions. Only then can we turn our hearts, minds, and lives towards him.

REFLECTIONS

_____

_____

_____

_____

_____

_____

Distractions and demands have a way of scattering us, so that it is not uncommon for us to be doing one thing and thinking of another. We are not wholly present to what is at hand and if we live most of the hours of the day like this, the pattern will follow us into our time of prayer.

— Flannery O'Connor

And he said, "Jesus, remember me when you come into your kingdom".
Luke 23:42

REMEMBER ME LORD

As he was dying, our Lord revealed that there is an arena beyond this life. Life after death does not depend on what we have done, but on whether we humbly open our hearts in love with the words too deep for explanation, "Lord, remember me." Representing the two sides of our heart, the two thieves embodied shame and fear on one hand and love and humility on the other. Which side of our heart is victorious depends on which side we choose to feed.

REFLECTIONS

_____

_____

_____

_____

_____

_____

If ever there is tomorrow when we're not together... there is something you must always remember. You are braver than you believe, stronger than you seem, and smarter than you think. But the most important thing is, even if we're apart... I'll always be with you.
— A.A. Milne

AUGUST

In life, we cannot do great things. We can only do small things with great love.

— Mother Teresa

AUGUST 1

Truly, truly, I say to you, unless a grain of wheat falls into the earth and dies, it remains alone; but if it dies, it bears much fruit.

John 12:24

FROM RECOVERY TO DISCOVERY

If we are going to move to discovery, we need to love by design – deliberately opening our innermost selves to accept love, even when pain seems to overcome us. Love is not just a sense of feeling ecstatic or walking in nirvana. Love is a result of the commitment to work through the pain and hurt in our lives so we can open more space in our hearts to love, beauty, and truth. Unfortunately, we sometimes substitute distorted love for the real love of God.

REFLECTIONS

_____

_____

_____

_____

_____

The only journey is the one within.

— Rainer Maria Rilke

AUGUST 2

Lord, they have killed your prophets, they have demolished your altars, and I alone am left, and they seek my life.

Romans 11:3

THE CAPTAIN OF OUR SHIP

Without a true focus on the worship of the Holy Other, we are totally thrown upon ourselves to become the captain of our ship and the master of our fate. This enormous responsibility forces us to become our own god. But God is all powerful and all knowing. Therefore, to be our own god, we have to know everything, win every battle and be in total control. This of course is ridiculous. Eventually we find ourselves angry, burned out, fatigued, and depressed.

REFLECTIONS

_____

_____

_____

_____

_____

_____

No one is useless in this world who lightens the burdens of another.

— Charles Dickens

Draw near to God, and he will draw near to you. Cleanse your hands, you sinners, and purify your hearts, you double-minded.

James 4:8

THE PRINCIPLE OF SIMPLICITY

Christ's life embodied the principle of simplicity. He was always clothed in humility and never double-minded. Pure devotion and childlike wonder can be crowded out by the complexities of adult life. We have to make room in our hearts for simple truth, love, and spirituality. But note that Christ did not give up his identity, his calling, or his ability to do something significant.

Some people equate simplicity with the olden days, and in these people's minds "the olden days" mean regression. But this simplicity I speak of has nothing to do with the retreat to primitive ways of the past but the simplicity of living as 'the beloved child of God'.

REFLECTIONS

_____

_____

_____

_____

_____

_____

Our life is frittered away by detail. Simplify, simplify.

— Henry David Thoreau

August 4

For the wages of sin is death, but the free gift of God is eternal life in Christ Jesus our Lord.

Romans 6:23

Turning Back to God

Contemplation is turning from the things of God to the presence of God. Held by God's love, contemplation is a transformation of consciousness that motivates us to carry out the mission of love in the world. Although we may prepare for contemplation through any number of spiritual and psychological practices, contemplation, the awareness of the presence and communion with God, is a grace, a gift. We do not start at contemplation, we arrive there.

Reflections

Our love is a need, his is a gift. We need to see good in ourselves in order to love ourselves. He does not. He loves us not because we are good but because He is.

— Thomas Merton

And calling the crowd to him with his disciples, he said to them, "If anyone would come after me, let him deny himself and take up his cross and follow me".

Mark 8:34

THE MYTH OF NARCISSUS

Discussing the myth of Narcissus in *The Fall of Public Man*, Richard Sennet warns that the myth is not only about the danger of self-love, but that Narcissus was so absorbed with the reflection of his own image that he failed to recognize the water as "other" and fell in and was drowned. Self-absorption prevents us from recognizing and relating to the other. To Rudolph Otto, in his important book *Idea of the Holy*, God is the *"Wholly Other"*. And so our god or pseudo god, like the reflection of Narcissus, becomes a projection of ourselves.

REFLECTIONS

_____

_____

_____

_____

_____

_____

Since [narcissists] deep down, feel themselves to be faultless, it is inevitable that when they are in conflict with the world they will invariably perceive the conflict as the world's fault. Since they must deny their own badness, they must perceive others as bad. They project their own evil onto the world. They never think of themselves as evil; on the other hand, they consequently see much evil in others.

— M. Scott Peck

AUGUST 6

Their land is filled with idols; they bow down to the work of their hands,
to what their own fingers have made.

Isaiah 2:8

PSYCHOLOGICAL REDUCTIONISM

My thesis is that in this era of psychological reductionism we are driven inward, having lost faith in political ideologies and other processes around us. Confronting a deep sense of inadequacy because of the overwhelming challenges facing us, we become self-absorbed and create powerful, unconscious images of ourselves. Seeking tangible forms of meaning for our lives, we become vulnerable to create idols and pseudo gods by projecting our narcissistic images onto surrounding reality. In essence, our idols and pseudo gods are projections of ourselves.

REFLECTIONS

When we cease to worship God, we do not worship nothing, we worship anything.

— G.K. Chesterton

AUGUST 7

For as I passed along and observed the objects of your worship, I found also an altar with this inscription, 'To the unknown god.' What therefore you worship as unknown, this I proclaim to you.

Acts 17:23

TRANSCENDENT UNCERTAINTY

In spite of the uncertainty in our lives, our search is the same. We long to connect to the transcendent, the eternal mystery, in seeking meaning for our life. In Christianity, the incarnation means that God the transcendent has become a part of us. His name is now God-for-us. He was with us in the past, is with us now, and will be with us forever.

REFLECTIONS

_____

_____

_____

_____

_____

_____

We cannot be satisfied forever by the guesses of yesterday, however the charm of tradition and ritual may, for a time, lull our doubts about their validity. We must hammer away until we have forged a clear and valid picture not only of this vast universe in which we live but also of our very selves.

— Francis Crick

August 8

Their end is destruction, their god is their belly, and they glory in their shame, with minds set on earthly things.

Philippians 3:19

Man-Made gods

In ancient times idols were human made images of people, animals, or other objects worshiped as gods. The images were often made of wood, clay, or stone and sometimes covered with precious metals or jewels. Some natural sites, for example, mountains or other high places were worshiped as a dwelling place of the gods. In the New Testament idols were associated with various human appetites such as coveting, lust, or greed. In essence, an idol is anything that is given ultimate value and worshiped in place of God the holy One. God warned that we should have no other gods beside him.

Reflections

_____

_____

_____

_____

_____

_____

Idolatry is the practice of ascribing absolute value to things of relative worth.

— Frederick Buechner

August 9

The God who made the world and everything in it, being Lord of heaven and earth, does not live in temples made by man.

Acts 17:24

Technological Sterility

In modern culture, however, the situation is more confusing because the concept of idolatry or pseudo gods is less well-defined. Why is this so? I am not sure. There is no doubt, however, that our technological achievements and so-called sophisticated way of life have reduced the mystery of life. Yet great is the mystery of godliness. We can only appreciate that mystery by accepting the indwelling presence of God in our life.

Reflections

_____

_____

_____

_____

_____

_____

The approach to and understanding of what an Idol is begins with the understanding of what God is not. God, as a supreme value and goal, is not man, the state, and institution, nature, power, possession, sexual powers or any artifacts made by man."

— Erich Fromm

AUGUST 10

All worshipers of images are put to shame, who make their boast in worthless idols; worship him, all you gods!

Psalm 97:7

IDOL WORSHIP

Idolatry is an age-old phenomenon that is often mistakenly relegated to a thing of the past. In fact, Neo-Freudian analyst Erich Fromm said that the history of mankind is primarily the history of idol worship, from the primitive idols of clay and wood to the modern idols of the state, leaders, production, and consumption. In a Judeo- Christian context, idolatry is defined as a worship of anything besides God, the supreme being of the universe who is immortal, ultimate, transcendent, and imminent.

REFLECTIONS

_____

_____

_____

_____

_____

_____

Whatever is begun in anger, ends in shame.

— Benjamin Franklin

August 11

Anyone who does not love does not know God, because God is love.

1 John 4:8

God is love

God, in love, reached out to us through his son Jesus Christ to deliver us from the futility and destruction of our false selves. Jesus reminds us that if we are to follow him, we must deny ourselves (our false selves), take up our crosses (face the reality of our pain and failure before God) and follow him (accept his sacrifice and forgiveness). Only then will we find our true selves in God. This is a continual challenge for all of us, but it is the essence of life.

Reflections

_____

_____

_____

_____

_____

_____

The Christian does not think God will love us because we are good, but that God will make us good because He loves us.

— C.S. Lewis

August 12

My beloved is mine, and I am his; he grazes among the lilies.

Song of Solomon 2:16

Beloved of God

According to the Judeo-Christian perspective, we are made in the image of God. God is love, which involves the good (doing), the true (knowing), and the beautiful (feeling). Our true essence is to live in love. We come from love, to be loved, and return to love. Life then is the cosmic dance of love with God, the Hound of Heaven, seeking us, the beloved. Sometimes it is hard to receive God's love becasue where we expected love, we received pain. As a result, we fear opening up to love because we might be hurt again.

Reflections

_____

_____

_____

_____

_____

_____

The root of Christian love is not the will to love but the faith that one is loved.

— Thomas Merton

Now Sarai was barren; she had no children.

Genesis 11:30

CONTENTIOUS SARAI

Abraham had a deep, loving relationship with his beautiful wife Sarah. Sarah started off her life being called Sarai, which means contentious. But as she continued her journey to God, he changed her name to Sarah, meaning princess. Life is about growing our souls and Sarah's growth through the grace of her spiritual journey is an excellent example, challenging us to move from a contentious to a serene spirit.

REFLECTIONS

_____

_____

_____

_____

_____

_____

In all of us there is a hunger, marrow-deep, to know our heritage- to know who we are and where we have come from. Without this enriching knowledge, there is a hollow yearning. No matter what our attainments in life, there is still a vacuum, an emptiness, and the most disquieting loneliness.

— Alex Haley

AUGUST 14

And Sarah died at Kiriath-arba (that is, Hebron) in the land of Canaan, and Abraham went in to mourn for Sarah and to weep for her.

Genesis 23:2

GRIEVING SARAH

It is very touching how Abraham grieved – he came to mourn for Sarah to weep for her. In those days corpses were put in a special tent and the bereaved husband knelt down before the corpse. Grieving for Sarah, Abraham knelt down and gave thanks and appreciation for the faithfulness and commitment of his dear wife. Most touching of all is the fact that even though Abraham was offered Sarah's tomb free of charge, he refused to accept it becasue he valued his love for her very deeply.

REFLECTIONS

_____

_____

_____

_____

_____

_____

Live, then, and be happy, beloved children of my heart, and never forget, that until the day God will deign to reveal the future to man, all human wisdom is contained in these two words, "Wait and Hope."

— Alexandre Dumas

August 15

You will have your fill of shame instead of glory. Drink, yourself, and show your uncircumcision! The cup in the Lord's right hand will come around to you, and utter shame will come upon your glory!

Habakuk 2:16

Shame

Jesus told his disciples that he was going away, but that when they received each other they were receiving him. How important it is to recognize that in our spiritual journey, Jesus often comes to us in other people. Shame prevents us from recognizing the visitation of Christ in others. Only when we transcend our shame can we see Christ in the people around us. Christ is in our midst in spite of all our hurt and pain. He is the immanent reality that blesses and renews us.

Reflections

_____

_____

_____

_____

_____

_____

Heaven knows we need never be ashamed of our tears, for they are rain upon the blinding dust of earth, overlying our hard hearts. I was better after I had cried, than before--more sorry, more aware of my own ingratitude, more gentle.

— Charles Dickens, *Great Expectations*

AUGUST 16

Blessed is the one who listens to me, watching daily at my gates, waiting beside my doors.

Proverbs 8:34

THE PROMISE DELAYED

Abraham wanted to buy the tomb as a statement of faith that his descendants would inherit the land. During his lifetime, the only land that Abraham owned was the land he bought for Sarah's tomb. As Abraham counted all the pieces of silver and bought the tomb, he powerfully demonstrated his love and commitment. So often in our lives we do not see the fulfillment of God's promise. Our challenge is to live in faith and hope, by serving God and bowing to Him. God will fulfill his promises for us in his own time and place.

REFLECTIONS

_____

_____

_____

_____

_____

_____

Waiting is painful. Forgetting is painful. But not knowing which to do is the worst kind of suffering.

— Paulo Coelho

August 17

As for me, I shall behold your face in righteousness; when I awake, I shall be satisfied with your likeness.

Psalm 17:15

Called to God

How important it is for us to realize that God calls us to himself as an antidote to fear. Reminding us that he is the one who really protects us, he also warns us and encourages us to recognize that he himself, and he alone, is our reward. In other words, we seek God who gives us consolation, rather than seeking consolation and finding God. God himself is the desire of our hearts. We all long to see the face of God, for it is in his image that we are made. We belong to God.

Reflections

_____

_____

_____

_____

_____

I do not think that all who choose wrong roads perish; but their rescue consists in being put back on the right road. A sum can be put right: but only by going back til you find the error and working it afresh from that point, never by simply going on. Evil can be undone, but it cannot 'develop' into good. Time does not heal it. The spell must be unwound, bit by bit, 'with backward mutters of dissevering power' --or else not.

— C.S. Lewis, *The Great Divorce*

AUGUST 18

After these things the word of the Lord came to Abram in a vision: "Fear not, Abram, I am your shield; your reward shall be very great".

Genesis 15:1

TESTING

God is love. As we continue to journey toward contemplation, like Abraham, we will journey to our own Mount Moriah, the place of challenge and testing. Some of us may be going through this experience at this very moment. May God give us grace to experience his presence and love. The testing of our faith is very difficult and lonely, but God is with us. Earlier on in Abraham's life, when he felt discouraged and maybe afraid after conquering the Kings of Salem, God spoke to him so beautifully saying,"Fear not, Abram, for I am your shield; your reward shall be very great".

REFLECTIONS

_____

_____

_____

_____

_____

_____

*Time is
Too Slow for those who Wait,
Too Swift for those who Fear,
Too Long for those who Grieve,
Too Short for those who Rejoice;
But for those who Love,
Time is not."*
— Henry van Dyke

From there he moved to the hill country on the east of Bethel and pitched his tent, with Bethel on the west and Ai on the east. And there he built an altar to the Lord and called upon the name of the Lord.

Genesis 12:8

LIFE IS TRANSITORY

Arriving in Canaan, Abraham built an altar to worship God and pitched a tent. The altar and the tent are both characteristic of the spiritual journey. The altar represents a commitment to giving God the supreme place in our lives. The altar is a place where we meet God, the place where we call upon God, the place where we respond to the call of God. The tent reminds us that life is transitory and that we are on a journey. No matter who we are and what we do or accomplish, we live in a tent. Life comes and goes...so do we!

REFLECTIONS

_____

_____

_____

_____

_____

_____

We must be willing to let go of the life we planned so as to have the life that is waiting for us.

— Joseph Campbell

August 20

So he built an altar there and called upon the name of the Lord and pitched his tent there. And there Isaac's servants dug a well.

Genesis 26:25

A Mausoleum for a Tent

Whenever we replace God on the altar of our lives, we create idols or addictions. Whenever we replace the tent and forget that life is transitory, we create a mausoleum, a kind of death in the midst of life. It may be a beautiful home or great business but without the context of the altar and the recognition of the tent, it is death in the midst of life. Knowing God or moving into deeper spirituality, which I define as contemplation, involves respecting God on the altar of our lives and remembering that we live in a tent.

Reflections

_____

_____

_____

_____

_____

_____

Still round the corner there may wait
A new road or a secret gate
And though I oft have passed them by
A day will come at last when I
Shall take the hidden paths that run
West of the Moon, East of the Sun.

— J.R.R. Tolkien

August 21

Who died for us so that whether we are awake or asleep we might live with him.

1 Thessalonians 5:10

Called to Contemplation

So often when things become difficult in our lives, we run away. Opening ourselves to God's presence, we often hear him telling us to return to where we belong, that is, to go back to the first things, our faith, our simple prayer life, our church, or back to our fellowship. Often there is pain, but when God calls us to go back, he is not necessarily calling us to the dynamics of situation or persons involved. He is calling us to himself. Contemplation means living our lives in God's presence, the eternal now.

Reflections

_____

_____

_____

_____

_____

_____

Once you have tasted flight, you will forever walk the earth with your eyes turned skyward, for there you have been, and there you will always long to return.

— Leonardo da Vinci

AUGUST 22

Then the Lord appeared to Abram and said, "To your offspring I will give this land." So he built there an altar to the Lord, who had appeared to him.

Genesis 12:7

ABRAHAM'S ALTAR

In a very deep sense, contemplation means a willingness to be tested by God. God called Abraham to face a test of authenticity of his altar, that is His ultimate concern. God is always testing our altar, because the altar is the place where our true selves abide in God. Without the altar, we succumb to our false selves, which are associated with illusive programs for happiness, idols and addictions. The altar must be kept intact because without it we forget that we live in a tent, and we create an illusion of permanence.

REFLECTIONS

Upon the altar of God I pledge eternal hostility against every form of tyranny over the mind of man.

— Thomas Jefferson

And Isaac said to his father Abraham, "My father!" And he said, "Here I am, my son." He said, "Behold, the fire and the wood, but where is the lamb for a burnt offering?" Abraham said, "God will provide for himself the lamb for a burnt offering, my son."

Genesis 22:7-8

A PAINFUL JOURNEY

In the story God asked Abraham to sacrifice his beloved heir Isaac. This is mystery and we can only imagine the pain and conflict experienced by Abraham. But, being faithful, Abraham obeyed God and took his son, his only son Isaac, to Mount Moriah to sacrifice him, perhaps in some way hoping that God would redeem even the most tragic circumstances. The journey to Mount Moriah is always a painful process in our lives. But sadly, no one can go into a deeper experience of contemplation or spirtuality without walking their journey to Mount Moriah. Have you expereinced your Mount Moriah?

REFLECTIONS

_____

_____

_____

_____

_____

_____

When you love you wish to do things for. You wish to sacrifice for. You wish to serve.

— Ernest Hemingway

August 24

Then Abraham reached out his hand and took the knife to slaughter his son. But the angel of the Lord called to him from heaven and said, "Abraham, Abraham!" And he said, "Here I am." He said, "Do not lay your hand on the boy or do anything to him, for now I know that you fear God, seeing you have not withheld your son, your only son, from me."

Genesis 22:10-12

A Mount Moriah Moment

Sometimes our Mount Moriah may involve a particular illness, the failure of a business, depression, or some kind of problem with our children or family. However, all of us, some way or the other, as we open ourselves to the deeper aspect of our spiritual journey, will find our way to Mount Moriah. Even our Lord Jesus Christ in the Garden of Gethsemane, cried, "My father, if it is possible, may this cup be taken from me. Yet not as I will, but as you will" (Matthew 26:39).

Reflections

_____

_____

_____

_____

_____

_____

But sometimes illumination comes to our rescue at the very moment when all seems lost; we have knocked at every door and they open on nothing until, at last, we stumble unconsciously against the only one through which we can enter the kingdom we have sought in vain a hundred years - and it opens.

— Marcel Proust, *In Search of Lost Time*

AUGUST 25

My sould waits in silence for God and Him alone.

Psalm 62:1

SPIRITUAL MATURITY

At a certain point Abraham came to the place on the journey to Mount Moriah where he told those accompanying him to stay put while he and his son went forth to worship. Abraham called the testing of God worship (Genesis 22:5). This is always a sign of deep spiritual maturity. Worship is the only grace we have in life. It is the duty of all human beings because in this life we can never be satisfied or experience God fully, unless we worship. In the midst of these two forces we are called upon to worship God and to glorify him forever. As we worship God, we acknowledge that we are made in his image. We recognize that he is in charge of our lives. As St. Augustine said, "We shall ever restless be until we find our rest in thee".

REFLECTIONS

_____

_____

_____

_____

_____

_____

The mark of the immature man is that he wants to die nobly for a cause, while the mark of the mature man is that he wants to live humbly for one.

— **J.D. Salinger**, *The Catcher in the Rye*

Draw near to God, and he will draw near to you. Cleanse your hands, you sinners, and purify your hearts, you double-minded.

James 4:8

CLARIFY AND PURIFY

The experience of testing is always to clarify and purify the presence of God in our lives and open our hearts for worship. Worship is the screening process that God uses on our lives to separate out the dross of the false self attachments and addictions, leaving us to experience our true selves in God. At the time of testing it is important to call upon the God of all comfort, and to realize that he is calling us unto himself in worship, to experience being alone with the Alone, the one and only true God.

REFLECTIONS

_____

_____

_____

_____

_____

_____

Peace demands the most heroic labor and the most difficult sacrifice. It demands greater heroism than war. It demands greater fidelity to the truth and a much more perfect purity of conscience.

— Thomas Merton

For we do not have a high priest who is unable to sympathize with our weaknesses, but one who in every respect has been tempted as we are, yet without sin.

Hebrews 4:15

DISCOURAGEMENT

Sometimes testing discourages us; it may or may not be followed by growth. God tests us in order to bless us and to reveal the ministry of his love to us. Faithful to God's test, Abraham is promised a special blessing for himself, his family, his descendants, in fact the whole world. If we are willing to walk faithfully with God in our testing, he purifies our hearts and opens us to deeper blessings.

REFLECTIONS

_____

_____

_____

_____

_____

_____

Iron rusts from disuse, stagnant water loses its purity, and in cold weather becomes frozen; even so does inaction sap the vigors of the mind.

— Leonardo da Vinci

August 28

Blessed are the pure in heart, for they will see God.

Matthew 5:8

The Pure in Heart

Contemplation always involves purification which places our hearts under the scrutiny of God's piercing eyes to remove our selfishness. This allows us to experience our total dependence on Him. Most importantly, in testing Abraham, God was revealing a blueprint for the redemption of the world through the sacrificial death of his son, the Lord Jesus Christ. Taking Abraham into his confidence, God was revealing the ultimate hope for the renewal of the world.

Reflections

Always aim at complete harmony of thought and word and deed. Always aim at purifying your thoughts and everything will be well.

— Mahatma Gandhi

August 29

After these things God tested Abraham and said to him, "Abraham!"
And he said, "Here I am." He said, "Take your son, your only son Isaac,
whom you love, and go to the land of Moriah, and offer him there as a
burnt offering on one of the mountains of which I shall tell you."

Genesis 22:1-2

Sacrifice

As Abraham was about to sacrifice Isaac, the angel stopped his hand and a lamb was provided. God was showing Abraham that he would give his son Jesus Christ, but at that point there would be no hand to stop the onslaught of the cruel crown of thorns, the piercing spear, the beating and the shame. Seeing Jesus, John the Baptist announced, "Behold the Lamb of God that takes away the sin of the world" (John 1:29). Jesus the Savior of the world died for our sins, but he also rose triumphantly from the grave, conquering death and bringing hope and salvation to the world.

Testing is never easy, but it must be seen in the context of God, who is love revealing himself to us, the beloved.

Reflections

As my sufferings mounted I soon realized that there were two ways in which I could respond to my situation -- either to react with bitterness or seek to transform the suffering into a creative force. I decided to follow the latter course.

— Martin Luther King Jr.

AUGUST 30

Where there is no prophetic vision the people are discouraged.

Proverbs 29:18

THE VISION OF GOD

Contemplation involves an appreciation of the vision of God, followed by the sincere commitment to serve the mission of God's love in the world. To have the vision without the mission is an empty experience, producing a sense of frustration and misguidance. The mission of love without the vision of God in the world produces busyness and burnout.

REFLECTIONS

_____

_____

_____

_____

_____

_____

You know that this is the compulsiveness that keeps us going and busy, but at the same time makes us wonder whether we are getting anywhere in the long run. This is the way to spiritual exhaustion and burn-out. This is the way to spiritual death.

— Henri J.M. Nouwen

Therefore shall the protection of Pharaoh turn to your shame, and the shelter in the shadow of Egypt to your humiliation.

Isaiah 30:3

HUMILIATION

The fear of abandonment, rejection, and humiliation is so effective that many of us are more influenced by fear than by love. Living in love is more open but it makes us more vulnerable. Fear, on the other hand, encourages illusions, isolation, and intimacy dysfunction. With increasing threats of terrorism, crime and violence, more people seem to be living in the house of fear, rather than in the house of love.

REFLECTIONS

_____

_____

_____

_____

_____

_____

If you want to be respected by others, the great thing is to respect yourself. Only by that, only by self-respect will you compel others to respect you.

— Fyodor Dostoyevsky, *The Insulted and Humiliated*

September

One ought, everyday at least, to hear a little song, read a good poem, see a fine picture and if it were possible, to speak a few reasonable words.

— Johann Wolfgang Von Goethe

September 1

How long will you love delusions and seek false gods?

Psalm 4:2

Open to the Lie

Focusing on what is least substantial, the false self turns away from what is real, creating a world of illusion. It is very humbling to recognize that there is a tendency in our hearts to be more open to the lie or the reconstruction of reality than to accept reality itself. The false self creates illusions to make us feel better. The false self, in seeking to make us feel better, will even negotiate hurting ourselves in suicide or hurting others in homicide. Thomas Merton said that everyone is shadowed by an illusory person: a false self. We are not very good at recognizing illusions, least of all the ones we cherish about ourselves.

Reflections

_____

_____

_____

_____

_____

_____

Whatever your heart clings to and confides in, that is really your God, your functional savior.

— Martin Luther

September 2

Have I not commanded you? Be strong and courageous. Do not be frightened, and do not be dismayed, for the Lord your God is with you wherever you go.

Joshua 1:9

Courage for the Journey

As we use bandages to cover physical wounds, so the false self hides the wounds of our inadequacies. This prevents us from being authentically observed by others. All of us have been hurt to some extent in childhood or at some other time in our life, leaving us with powerful feelings of abandonment, rejection, shame, grief and anger. Our false selves are developed by our brains to compensate for the traumas experienced in our lives. As a result, the false self uses such defenses as denial, pleasing others (codependency), blaming others (projection), overworking and various types of addictions to coverup our underlying hurts. It is only when we have the courage to make the journey to our hearts and face the painful experiences of our inner lives that we can empty our hearts of hurt and pain. In so doing, our true selves surface, making us authentic.

Reflections

_____

_____

_____

_____

_____

_____

Courage is the first of human qualities because it is the quality which guarantees all the others.

— Winston Churchill

SEPTEMBER 3

But the Lord is in his holy temple; let all the earth keep silence before him.

Habakuk 2:20

DREAD OF SILENCE

Blocked from intimacy with God, ourselves, and others, the false self produces internal resistance to prayer. Creating an existential dread of silence and being alone with God, the false self specializes in distractions and illusions. It encourages laziness, sloth and resistance in our spiritual life, producing form without substance.

REFLECTIONS

_____

_____

_____

_____

_____

_____

The tiny Lilliputians surmise that Gulliver's watch may be his god, because it is that which, he admits, he seldom does anything without consulting.

— Jonathan Swift, *Gulliver's Travels*

SEPTEMBER 4

*When the Lamb opened the seventh seal, there was **silence** in heaven for about half an hour.*

Revelation 8:1

THE SOUNDS OF SILENCE

Silence within and without is unnerving. Silence confronts the false self with its own nothingness and leads to its undoing. To avoid silence we may fill our days with activity and noise. We can fall asleep and wake up to the sound of the radio. We have smart phones that play videos and connect us to the noise of the Internet. Satellites feed music to our vehicles 24/7. We walk with our iPod ear buds firmly in place and when our walk is over, we return to the hundreds of cable channels on television. For some people a book is preferable to quietness. It is possible to live without constant noise, but in the absence of background distractions, we fear being faced with our own emptiness.

REFLECTIONS

_____

_____

_____

_____

_____

_____

And the people bowed and prayed
To the neon god they made
And the sign flashed out its warning
In the words that it was forming
And the sign said, "The words of the prophets are written
on the subway walls and tenement halls"
And whispered in the sounds of silence.

— Paul Simon & Art Garfunkel

Let us then with confidence draw near to the throne of grace, that we may receive mercy and find grace to help in time of need.

Hebrews 4:16

Intimacy Dysfunction

The false self makes the world a lonely place because we don't let others get too close to us in case they see through our false identities. If we let them come too close, they discover our lack of authenticity or emptiness. We keep people at a distance - this is intimacy dysfunction. True spirituality challenges us to die to the false self, which imprisons and forces us to serve it in varying degrees of misery. Judeo-Christian tradition teaches that human beings are created in the image of God, who in essence, is the good, the true, and the beautiful. In our highest state we are reflectors of the good, the true, and the beautiful.

Reflections

_____

_____

_____

_____

_____

_____

The man who learns in solitude and recollection, to be at peace with his own loneliness, and to prefer its reality to the illusion of merely natural companionship, comes to know the invisible companionship of God.

— Thomas Merton

September 6

There is a way that seems right unto a man, but the end thereof is death.
Proverbs 16:25

The Limitation of the False Self

The false self is limited by time and space, and forces us to live only in that dimension. As a result, it buries our desires for the fulfillment of our spirit and encourages us to feed on our accomplishments, the admiration and affirmation of others. It is totally ego-centric. Ego stands for Escorting God Out. This means that we are left to suffer the illusion of being the masters of our own fate and the architect of our independence and self-sufficiency. The false self is entirely unsubstantial, lacking in fullness of being, and cannot survive death. Consequently, we develop an illusion of permanence, finding ourselves living by greed, materialism and control. It is only by embracing the stillness of silence that we discover the authenticity of our true self and the presence of God.

Reflections

Sometimes people put up walls, not to keep others out, but to see who cares enough to break them down.

— Author Unknown

But if your eye is bad, your whole body will be full of darkness. If then the light in you is darkness, how great is the darkness!

Matthew 6:23

Beyond the Senses

Contemplation opens us to true communion, which often involves the mystical aspects of life; knowing beyond knowing, seeing beyond seeing, hearing beyond hearing, which is nevertheless as real as the rational cognitive approach. As we combine these two forms of knowing – the cognitive and intuitive – we come to understand more of what it means to be human. As a result we discover the way to transcendence, love, freedom, inner peace, and unity in the midst of diversity.

Reflections

_____

_____

_____

_____

_____

_____

The eye through which I see God is the same eye through which God sees me; my eye and God's eye are one eye, one seeing, one knowing, one love.

— Meister Eckhart

SEPTEMBER 8

I desire then that in every place men should pray, lifting up holy hands without anger or quarreling;

1 Timothy 2:8

ADDICTIVE SELF-IMAGE

Our natural tendency in the face of crisis is to revert into our addictive self-image and familiar old self -soothing patterns of the false self. However, we can take as our model Mary Magdalene at the tomb of Jesus. She just stayed there. It was painful, but she stayed there. She was alone and griving, but she stayed there. It seemed as if the situation was hopeless, but she stayed there. She was told that in some sense Christ was not there, but she stayed there. The disciples left having found the tomb empty, but Mary stayed there. The only way out of the crisis is a determined commitment to stay focused on the Word of God in silence. Mary's separation and individuation opened her to the revelation of the risen Lord. She was the first to know that the party of life had begun, because in the resurrection, shame and death were destroyed.

REFLECTIONS

_____

_____

_____

_____

_____

_____

I have been driven many times upon my knees by the overwhelming conviction that I had no where else to go. My own wisdom and that of all about me seemed insufficient for that day.

— Abraham Lincoln

September 9

And we know that for those who love God all things work together for good, for those who are called according to his purpose.

Romans 8:28

Seeing God in All Things

An early and important insight that results from our prayer life is that as our spirituality broadens, we open ourselves to seeing God's presence in all persons and situations, hence experiencing the infinite freedom of His love. In truth, authentic spirituality is the expansion of the inner self, i.e., the soul, to a limitless universe. In reality, because life is wounded this awareness is not complete, and our false selves can easily block it out as they seek to defend us against the pains of life.

Reflections

_____

_____

_____

_____

_____

_____

Dwell on the beauty of life. Watch the stars, and see yourself running with them.

— Marcus Aurelius

September 10

The things that are seen are temporal, but the things that are unseen are eternal.

2 Corinthians 4:18

Cultivating the Ability to See

Contemplative spirituality cultivates the ability to see not only with our eyes, but with the eyes of our heart. When we see with the eyes of our heart, we understand and open ourselves to the authentic presence of God in our lives. The eyes are purely for physiological seeing, but our heart is the organ for meaning. Therefore, when we see with the eyes of the heart, we not only see physiologically, but we open to the deeper meaning of the mystery of life and spirituality.

Reflections

_____

_____

_____

_____

_____

_____

Don't think, look.
— Wittgenstin

What then shall we say to these things? If God is for us, who can be against us?

Romans 8:31

THE TRUE "I"

Our "I" can never be characterized: I am rich, I am poor, I am educated, I am uneducated. I'm still the same person. The essential person is the same because we are made in the image of the Eternal Being. This reality allows us to face life with courage, hope, and love, recognizing that although we may not have what we want, or have not achieved our goals in life, we are still defined by God's love. This gives us new meaning and purpose to our life, in both the temporal and eternal perspectives.

REFLECTIONS

_____

_____

_____

_____

_____

_____

This above all: to thine own self be true,
And it must follow, as the night the day,
Thou canst not then be false to any man.
— William Shakespeare, *Hamlet*

SEPTEMBER 12

This is the message we have heard from him and proclaim to you, that God is light, and in him is no darkness at all.

1 John 1:5

WALKING IN THE LIGHT

Certainly once I know that I am embraced by the divine creative love and loved by love itself, which is the source of all there is, then I will never again see myself created by what others think. If I am no longer concerned about what others think, it is only because I want our relationship to exist in the domain of truth to be authentic and not false. This is discovery, or what the Scriptures call "walking in the light."

REFLECTIONS

There is a beautiful transparency to honest disciples who never wear a false face and do not pretend to be anything but who they are.

—Brennan Manning

SEPTEMBER 13

May you be strengthened with all power, according to his glorious might, for all endurance and patience with joy.

Colossians 1:11

RADIATING GOD'S LOVE

Our life can be likened to a bicycle wheel. When I live at the center (hub), that is my true self in God, then God's love radiates like spokes to the whole rim, touching all parts of my life. The test of our true selves in God is validated by the experience of deeper relationships and a sense of oneness with all other people. Our relationships with each other will be characterized by a sense of patience – that is learning to suffer with others and feel their pain, and a sense of kindness – learning to show mercy and forgiveness.

REFLECTIONS

_____

_____

_____

_____

_____

_____

Have courage for the great sorrows of life and patience for the small ones; and when you have laboriously accomplished your daily task, go to sleep in peace. God is awake.

— Victor Hugo

SEPTEMBER 14

*But the fruit of the Spirit is love, joy, peace, patience, kindness,
goodness, faithfulness. . . .*

Galatians 5:22

FAITHFULNESS

At its deepest level the true self also has important
personal qualities such as faithfulness. Faithfulness in both the
big and small things of life means learning to accept the
goodness of life, recognizing that good overcomes evil and love
overcomes hate. The true self is God living in us, rejuvenating
our being by His divine energy. When we awaken to our true
selves, it is painful to see our illusions shattered and
everything we built up crumble. This is the repentance that
changes our life. It is what I call 'discovery'.

REFLECTIONS

_____

_____

_____

_____

_____

*Any discussion of how pain and suffering fit into God's scheme ultimately
leads back to the cross.*

— Philip Yancey

I [meaning my false self] have been crucified with Christ; I no longer live, but Christ lives in me [my true self].

Galatians 2:20

COLLISION WITH REALITY

A sudden confrontation with reality destroys the false self. Christ is the ultimate reality and the revealer of the true self in all people. In the revelation of God's presence, the false self is destroyed and we experience our true selves in God. The result is the discovery of the 'abundant life' where there is no death, and we enter the cosmic dance with God, the Wholey Other.

REFLECTIONS

_____

_____

_____

_____

_____

_____

How many legs does a dog have if you call the tail a leg? Four. Calling a tail a leg doesn't make it a leg.

— Abraham Lincoln

SEPTEMBER 16

The fruit of the Spirit is love, joy, peace, patience, kindness, goodness, faithfulness, gentleness, and self-control; against such things there is no law.

Galatians 5:22-23

LOVE, PEACE AND JOY

To understand that God is constantly reaching out to us in love is heartwarming. He always comes. He comes in the thunder. He comes in the rain. He comes through people. He comes through circumstances. But he always comes to share His love, to share His peace, to share His joy. There will always be resistance, something to block our awareness of God's love. We can never be outside of His presence, but sadly, through our busyness and distractions, we can lose the awareness of His love. Let us stop today, and open to the awareness of God's love shining through the faces of our relatives, friends and even situations.

REFLECTIONS

When the doors of perception are cleansed, man will see things as they truly are, Infinite.

— William Blake

September 17

And no one puts new wine into old wineskins. If he does, the new wine will burst the skins and it will be spilled, and the skins will be destroyed.

Luke 5:37

New Wine

At the Last Supper, when Jesus was sharing intimate fellowship with his disciples, there was Judas, planning to destroy the whole process. But Jesus did not let this interfere with God's program. He still broke bread, took the cup and gave it to his disciples. He still washed the disciples' feet – even the feet of Judas. Evil is always present, but we should never give it power to block God's program.

Reflections

_____

_____

_____

_____

_____

_____

I find friendship to be like wine, raw when new, ripened with age, the true old man's milk and restorative cordial.

— Thomas Jefferson

SEPTEMBER 18

What then shall we say to these things? If God is for us, who can be against us?

Romans 8:31

SAFE AND SECURE

The human heart cries out for safety. When people feel safe they share their pain, let go of their anger, and give up their resentments. Contemplative prayer opens us to the presence and action of the external God in our lives. As a result we experience a sense of safety and relaxation, allowing our hearts to release hurts and pains embedded in our bodies. Contemplative prayer makes us safe as we open to the presence of the eternal God. As we relax and rest in his presence, our bodies and minds release and unload the hurts and wounds of a lifetime.

REFLECTIONS

_____

_____

_____

_____

_____

_____

What a blessedness, what a peace is mine,
Leaning on the everlasting arms.
Refrain: Leaning, leaning, safe and secure from all alarms;
— Anthony J. Showalter

September 19

Teach me, and I will be silent; make me understand how I have gone astray.

Job 6:24

Prayer of Silence

The sense of being loved is directly related to opening up to the prayer of silence. Silence is not just the absence of noise in the shutting down of communication with the outside world, but a process of coming to stillness. It is learning to be still and know the presence of God. Healing words come from silence, are accompanied by silence, and return to silence. Silence and solitude forge true and meaningful speech. Solitude does not mean physical isolation. Solitude is being alone with the Alone, experiencing the transcendent other, and growing in awareness of our identity as the beloved.

Reflections

_____

_____

_____

_____

_____

_____

Go placidly amid the noise and the haste, and remember what peace there may be in silence.

— Max Ehrmann, *Disiderata*

SEPTEMBER 20

When the crowds were increasing, he began to say, "This generation is an evil generation. It seeks for a sign, but no sign will be given to it except the sign of Jonah."

Luke 11:29

TRUE SILENCE

True silence always creates inner silence and inner silence always creates space: space for God, for ourselves, and for others. True solitude opens the door to the development of meaningful community. Without solitude we have isolation and loneliness and instead of creating community, we create a crowd. Contemplative prayer is the process of opening to our true selves and creating a meaningful solitude and community outside of our prayer time. Undoubtedly influenced by the small things that pull and tear at us, we so easily forget that we are the beloved.

REFLECTIONS

_____

_____

_____

_____

_____

_____

It is easy in the world to live after the world's opinion; it is easy in solitude to live after our own; but the great man is he who in the midst of the crowd keeps with perfect sweetness the independence of solitude.

— Ralph Waldo Emerson

SEPTEMBER 21

The unfolding of your words gives light; it imparts understanding to the simple.

Psalm 119:130

THE ART OF LISTENING

There are three levels of listening: phenomenal (surface), existential (problem-solving), and contemplative (communion). So often in our rushed lives we stay at the phenomenal level just listening on the surface, or maybe even at the existential level when we try to problem solve. But to understand the deeper levels of life, we have to reach the contemplative level. It's a place where we are required to wait patiently and listen in silence. It means listening another person into being and opening to the presence of God's love.

REFLECTIONS

_____

_____

_____

_____

_____

_____

The contemplative life is to retain with all one's mind the love of God and neighbor but to rest from exterior motion and cleave only to the desire of the Maker, that the mind may now take no pleasure in doing anything, but having spurned all cares may be aglow to see the face of its Creator.

— St. Gregory

September 22

Though you have not seen him, you love him. Though you do not now see him, you believe in him and rejoice with joy that is inexpressible and filled with glory.

1 Peter 1:8

BEING THE BELOVED

If I am not in touch with the realty that "I am the beloved", I cannot touch the sacredness of others. If I am a stranger to myself, I am likewise a stranger to others. The fact is we connect best with others when we connect with the core of ourselves. As we connect to the core of ourselves we touch the ground of our being that is God himself.

REFLECTIONS

_____

_____

_____

_____

_____

_____

When I allow God to liberate me from unhealthy dependence on people, I listen more attentively, love more unselfishly, and I am more compassionate and playful. I take myself less seriously, become aware that the breath of the father is on my face and my countenance is bright with laughter and a mystical adventure I thoroughly enjoy.

— Brennan Manning

And whenever you stand praying, forgive, if you have anything against anyone, so that your Father also who is in heaven may forgive you your trespasses.

Mark 11:25

THE COURAGE TO FORGIVE

Spending time in silent or contemplative prayer allows God to speak and act with greater strength in our lives. It gives us the freedom to forgive rather than to nurse the latest bruises of our wounded ego. It allows us to be capable of magnanimity during the petty moments of life; it empowers us to have courage despite the background tableaux of our fears and insecurities.

REFLECTIONS

_____

_____

_____

_____

_____

_____

Courage is contagious. When a brave man takes a stand, the spines of others are stiffened.

— Billy Graham

September 24

Likewise the Spirit helps us in our weakness. For we do not know what to pray for as we ought, but the Spirit himself intercedes for us with groanings too deep for words.

Romans 8:26

The Real

Many times when we practice deep, silent prayer, we become drowsy, but at the same time more energetic. It seems to me that the huge amount of energy expended by our false selves and the pursuit of illusory happiness is now available to be focused on things that really matter: love, friendship, and intimacy with God. Contemplation allows us to recognize that knowing God is living with the real in all that is real.

Reflections

_____

_____

_____

_____

_____

_____

Mother Teresa was asked, "How do you pray?" To which she replied, "I listen to God." Then she was asked, "What does God do?" And she said, "He listens to me."

— Mother Teresa

September 25

May their hearts be encouraged, being knit together in love, to reach all the riches of full assurance of understanding and the knowledge of God's mystery, which is Christ.

Colosians 2:2

The Mystery of Godliness

As we grasp the understanding of what it means to be present with God and open our true selves in him, we experience the mystery of God's presence. So often we speak glibly of knowing God, but it is very important for us to remember that great is the mystery of godliness. In His holy presence, we finite beings are hushed and trembling.

Reflections

Great indeed, we confess, is the mystery of godliness: He was manifested in the flesh, vindicated by the Spirit, seen by angels, proclaimed among the nations, believed on in the world, taken up in glory.

1 Timothy 3:16

SEPTEMBER 26

Blessed are the pure in heart, for they will see God.

Matthew 5:8

RISEN PRESENCE

The true self finds its basic security in an awareness of the presence of God in our lives. Jesus said that those with a pure heart will see God. To see the risen Christ is to move beyond the false self and open our hearts in every aspect of our lives. As we open to our true selves in God we experience the clarity and purity of His presence. This does not mean that we are perfect, without woundedness or sin. But it does mean an increased desire to worship, please and serve God.

REFLECTIONS

_____

_____

_____

_____

_____

_____

It is safe to tell the pure in heart that they shall see God, for only the pure in heart want to.

— C.S. Lewis

Their idols...have hands, but they cannot feel; they have feet, but they cannot walk; they cannot make a sound in their throat. Those who make them will become like them.

Psalm 115:4-8

PSEUDO GODS

Pseudo gods or idols are things and are not alive. God is a living God who is imminent and transcendent. The concept of idolatry is destructive, dehumanizing, and incompatible with true human freedom and redemption. Seducing us with the promise of ultimate fulfillment, pseudo gods exploit us. When they shatter, we are left distraught, abandoned and sometimes destroyed.

REFLECTIONS

We stand at a crossroads. Idolatry looms. Traditional values in jeopardy. Truth under siege and virtue abandoned.

— Gregory Maguire
*Wicked: The Life and Times
of the Wicked Witch of the West*

September 28

Since, then, you have been raised with Christ, set your hearts on things above.

Colossians 3:1

Projecting God Images

We can make an idol out of our faith in God. We tend to project onto God images from our own hearts. Freud has challenged us not to project onto God images of our earthly fathers, which causes God to become a projected defense of our oedipal strivings. In other words, we see God as our ideal father figure. J.B. Phillips suggests that a harsh and puritanical society will project its dominant qualities and create a harsh and puritanical God. Similarly, a lax and easygoing society will produce "a god with about as much moral authority as Father Christmas."

Reflections

_____

_____

_____

_____

_____

_____

Once God is seen as the Wholly Other reality out there, he can easily become a mere idol and a projection which enables human beings to externalize and worship their own prejudices and desires.

— Karen Armstrong

Do not be deceived: God is not mocked, for whatever one sows, that will he also reap.

Galatians 6:7

The Mockery of Faith

Often those of us who believe in God create a projected image of him, forcing him to fit into our existing box, schema, or image. Although we profess to know God, we actually worship a pseudo god or idol we ourselves have created. That is the worst type of idolatry because it produces a false arrogance, makes a mockery of faith, and blocks the image of the holy and beautiful in life.

Reflections

_____

_____

_____

_____

_____

_____

Images of the Holy easily become holy images—sacrosanct. My idea of God is not a divine idea. It has to be shattered time after time. He shatters it himself. He is the great iconoclast. Could we not almost say that this shattering is one of the marks of his presence?

— C.S. Lewis

September 30

Guard your heart for out of it flows the issues of your life.

Proverbs 4:23

The Holy Other

Idols and pseudo gods are made in our hearts. The heart is a metaphor for the center of our person. It is the real me or you. It is where all aspects of the person converge—the emotional, spiritual, social, cultural, and intellectual. It is the seat of our emotions, the place where good and evil interact in our lives. But it is, most of all, the place where God is, where the Holy Other relates to us.

Reflections

_____

_____

_____

_____

_____

_____

Every man becomes the image of the God he adores.
He whose worship is directed to a dead thing becomes dead.
He who loves corruption rots.
He who loves a shadow becomes, himself, a shadow.
He who loves things that must perish lives in dread of their perishing.

— Thomas Merton

October

Death is the stripping away of all that is not you. The secret of life is a "to die before you die" — and find that there is no death.

— Eckhart Tolle

October 1

For his invisible attributes, namely, his eternal power and divine nature, have been clearly perceived, ever since the creation of the world, in the things that have been made. So they are without excuse.

Romans 1:20

Projecting Guilt

The issues in our hearts are projected onto other people and onto God, the Holy Other. For example, a guilty person will project onto God a suspicious and disapproving image, creating a false god or pseudo god. In essence, knowing God means the willingness to work through the hurt and issues of our hearts so that we can move from projective issues of our hurt and issues of our hearts to come to know the real God.

Reflections

_____

_____

_____

_____

_____

_____

Although your mind works, your heart is darkened with depravity; and without a pure heart there can be no complete and true consciousness.

— Fyodor Dostoyevsky

October 2

You shall not make for yourself a carved image, or any likeness of anything that is in heaven above, or that is in the earth beneath, or that is in the water under the earth.

Exodus 20:4

In the Image of God

The only created image of God that the Scriptures recognize was made by God himself when he said, "Let us make man in our own image." Every other image is "less than God." When we do not view God as our ultimate concern, we make him a means and make a pseudo god of our faith. When we allow earthly things such as ideologies, or money, or any other objects to become ends in themselves, they become idols.

Reflections

_____

_____

_____

_____

_____

_____

The atheist staring from his attic window is often nearer to God than the believer caught up in his own false image of God.

— Martin Buber

October 3

The reason the Son of God appeared was to destroy the works of the devil.

1 John 3:8

Shattering the gods

Idols and pseudo gods are false and they must be shattered. The shattering may be a result of illness, disappointment, death, or some other tragedy, or the true God himself may demolish them. The shattering of one's pseudo gods is always painful, leaving a hole in one's soul and an emptiness of heart. We become vulnerable to depression, suicide, or other self-destructive actions like using drugs or alcohol. It is at these shattering points of extreme vulnerability that we can be open to true faith in God.

Reflections

_____

_____

_____

_____

_____

_____

Oh senseless man, who cannot possibly make a worm or a flea and yet will create Gods by the dozen!

— Michel de Montaigne

OCTOBER 4

You shall have no other gods before me.

Exodus 20:3

CHASING OTHER GODS

From Genesis to Revelation, the Bible proclaims idolatry to be an act of unfaithfulness. When Joshua led the Hebrews out of the wilderness and across the Jordan River into the Promised Land, God warned them against worshiping the gods of Canaan. They were commanded to destroy all of the idols of their conquered enemies. Those physical idols made of wood or bronze were easier to identify than idols such as money, appearance, popularity, and power.

REFLECTIONS

_____

_____

_____

_____

_____

_____

We always pay dearly for chasing after what is cheap.
— Aleksandr Solzhenitsyn

And the Word became flesh and dwelt among us, and we have seen his glory, glory as of the only Son from the Father, full of grace and truth.

John 1:14

Let God Be God

The coming of Christ, God incarnate, is the most powerful antidote to idolatry and pseudo gods. He came to dwell in us as God in the flesh so that we might not have to be our own god. I had a client who was an attorney. When the idol of his legal career shattered, he fell into hopelessness and despair. Through faith in Christ, he experienced a new depth of meaning and fulfillment in his life. He told me, "I am relieved that I don't have to be a god any longer."

Reflections

If God created us in his own image, we have more than reciprocated.

— Voltaire

I am the Alpha and the Omega," says the Lord God, "who is and who was and who is to come, the Almighty."

Revelation 1:8

THE TRANSCENDENT GOD

As human beings made in the image of God, we have the potential to give god status to anything. As worshiping creatures, our primary task is to put our problems in the proper perspective. No matter how difficult, they must be subjugated to our faith in God. Only then is there hope in the midst of our circumstances, for the true God is transcendent over the universe. Many of our problems need to be bowed before God to be put into their proper perspective. In so doing, we might be surprised to find that what appeared to be a problem was not a problem after all.

REFLECTIONS

_____

_____

_____

_____

_____

_____

You must live in the present, launch yourself on every wave, find your eternity in each moment. Fools stand on their island of opportunities and look toward another land. There is no other land; there is no other life but this.

— Henry David Thoreau

OCTOBER 7

Those who cling to wothless idols forfeit the grace that could be theirs.
Jonah 2:8

LIFE IS WOUNDED

There is an explanation for our constant creation of false gods. There is a reason we are forever shoving our faith aside and granting god-like status to both our pleasures and our problems. The reason is that life is wounded. There is an inextricable connection between our pain and our false gods.

REFLECTIONS

Men create gods after their own image, not only with regard to their form, but with regard to their mode of life.
— Aristotle

October 8

Now Adam knew Eve his wife, and she conceived and bore Cain, saying,
"I have gotten a man with the help of the Lord".

Genesis 4:1

A Rude Awakening

Imagine the first nine months of our life. What a wonderful life, floating in a tranquil sea with piped in water and food. Then the water rushed out and your paradise was shattered. Someone cut our lifeline and we lost our last connection to that utopian environment. We were then turned upside down and spanked. That should have been our first clue that life is wounded. It was nature's way of saying, "Go out there and live!" Unfortunately, even many years later, a lot of us still don't know how to live.

Reflections

_____

_____

_____

_____

_____

_____

He allowed himself to be swayed by his conviction that human beings
are not born once and for all on the day their mothers give birth to them,
but that life obliges them over and over again to give birth to
themselves.

— Gabriel Marcia Marquez

October 9

Yet you are he who took me from the womb; you made me trust you at my mother's breasts.

Psalm 22:9

Nature's Growth Cycle

In the aftershock of birth, we are comforted at the breast of our mother and all is well again. To our infant minds, there are no boundaries between us and our mothers. But as we grow, we begin to develop boundaries. All of sudden, we are no longer breast fed and psychologically we again feel like we are alone. This is the how we develop our identity. It is a natural cycle of comfort and then abandonment, where we are sent out again and again to grow. The reality is that there is no growth without suffering.

Reflections

_____

_____

_____

_____

_____

_____

Suffering has been stronger than all other teaching, and has taught me to understand what your heart used to be. I have been bent and broken, but - I hope - into a better shape.

— Charles Dickens

OCTOBER 10

For the Lord will not forsake his people; he will not abandon his heritage.
Psalm 94:14

FROM THE WOMB TO THE TOMB

Life is wounded and that woundedness does not stop when we grow beyond the struggles of childhood and adolescence. It does not cease when we pass it on to our sons and daughters. In fact, it grows worse. In spite of the golden promises of our society, many older citizens live in outright despair. Having done their best all their lives, the elderly often feel a sense of abandonment. From infancy to old age, we endure struggles. Life is wounded - it comes with the territory! The good news is that the resurrection is the antidote to our woundedness. It radiates hope and love throughout the stages of life...and even death.

REFLECTIONS

Do not abandon yourselves to despair. We are the Easter people and hallelujah is our song.

— Pope John Paul II

October 11

Every good gift and every perfect gift is from above, coming down from the Father of lights with whom there is no variation or shadow due to change.

James 1:17

Change and Loss

We all experience brokenness. Natural disasters like hurricanes, earthquakes, fires, and floods can destroy a lifetime of work, struggle and dedication in the blink of an eye. Politics, religion, the sudden death of a healthy young person, illness, and financial downturns all wound us and may leave us feeling abandoned and hopeless. In every aspect of existence, we see how life is forever changing. Where there is change, there is loss, and where there is loss, there is pain. In light of this painful reality, God is the unchanging core in a changing world!

Reflections

_____

_____

_____

_____

_____

_____

Any real change implies the breakup of the world as one has always known it, the loss of all that gave one an identity, the end of safety.

— James Baldwin

October 12

They abandoned the Lord and served the Baals and the Ashtaroth.

Judges 2:13

Pain and Anger

Like footprints on fresh cement, pain and hurt in childhood leave their mark. The continuing effect of pain on our lives is influenced by the intensity of the pain at the time of the trauma, by the stage of physical development, and by the amount of support available to the person during the pain. Pain is a complex issue, and unresolved pain from childhood or any other time in our life will cause problems later in life. Anger often accompanies pain and will linger until the wound which caused the pain is healed.

Reflections

_____

_____

_____

_____

_____

_____

Loss invites reflection and reformulating and a change of strategies. Loss hurts and bleeds and aches. Loss is always ready to call out your name in the night. Loss follows you home and taunts you at the breakfast table, follows you to work in the morning.

— Pat Conroy

OCTOBER 13

Search me, O God, and know my heart! Try me and know my thoughts!
Psalm 139:23

IN SEARCH OF THE HEART

As I explore my hurt, feeling its pain and confronting its causes, I learn that I am more able to help others remove their own masks and face their pain. Only as I search my own heart can I reach into the hearts of my friends and family. The search for the heart begins by following our hurt trail and the best companion we can take with us is God. He is the searcher of hearts and the comforter of souls.

REFLECTIONS

_____

_____

_____

_____

_____

_____

Tell your heart that the fear of suffering is worse than the suffering itself. And that no heart has ever suffered when it goes in search of its dreams, because every second of the search is a second's encounter with God and with eternity.

— Paulo Coelho, *Alchemist*

OCTOBER 14

No temptation has overtaken you that is not common to man. God is faithful, and he will not let you be tempted beyond your ability, but with the temptation he will also provide the way of escape, that you may be able to endure it.

1 Corinthians 10:13

UNIQUE AND UNIVERSAL

Although our problems are markedly different, we all share a wounded heart. We use different methods to deal with our hurt. Some of us become addicted to alcohol, and others isolate themselves or just drop out. Still others lose themselves in relationships, material possessions or career pursuits. Although our problems are diverse, the common denominator is that we are wounded. I have learned that my own woundedness is defended by my false self and the pseudo gods that I have worshiped. This is both personal to me and at the same time a universal truth.

REFLECTIONS

_____

_____

_____

_____

_____

_____

There is no insurmountable solitude. All paths lead to the same goal: to convey to others what we are.

— Pablo Neruda

To the woman he said, "I will surely multiply your pain in childbearing; in pain you shall bring forth children. Your desire shall be for your husband, and he shall rule over you."

Genesis 3:16

REPETITION COMPULSION

There is an old saying that "hurt people, hurt people." Psychology calls this the *repetition compulsion*. We repeat past pain in order to achieve some sense of mastery over it. Connected to this is the tendency of passing pain on to those who are, perhaps, weaker than we are. If parents don't work out their woundedness, they inevitably pass their pain on to their children. So often, children are forced to deal with the past pain of their parents rather than finding the joy of their own hearts.

REFLECTIONS

We are not necessarily doubting that God will do the best for us; we are wondering how painful the best will turn out to be.

— C.S. Lewis

October 16

The night racks my bones, and the pain that gnaws me takes no rest.

Job 30:17

Passing on Pain

Many people never learn to face themselves because they spend their whole lives working through their parents' issues. Our children don't need our money. They don't need to live in fancy houses or go to the best schools. They need our hearts — hearts that have been searched out by God and healed of the deep woundedness we all carry inside us. This does not mean that there are no more wounds, but that the woundedness is not being passed on, freeing the children to work on their own pain.

Reflections

_____

_____

_____

_____

_____

_____

You think your pain and your heartbreak are unprecedented in the history of the world, but then you read. It was books that taught me that the things that tormented me most were the very things that connected me with all the people who were alive, or who had ever been alive.

— James Baldwin

OCTOBER 17

Why do you hide your face and count me as your enemy?

Job 13:24

APPROACH AND AVOID

The wounded are afraid to love. Where we expected love as children we received pain. So, in our hearts we play a game that goes like this: if I avoid love, I avoid pain, yet, I still long to love and be loved. Therefore, I play "approach and avoid" to love. We have an alarming intimacy dysfunction in our culture. In one sense we get close to each other, but we don't want to get stuck. So we create distance, feel abandoned, then want to get close again. This makes committed love hard to understand. It takes a lot of courage to realize that we spend much of our time running away from the love that we yearn for!

REFLECTIONS

_____

_____

_____

_____

_____

_____

It has been said, 'time heals all wounds.' I do not agree. The wounds remain. In time, the mind, protecting its sanity, covers them with scar tissue and the pain lessens. But it is never gone.

— Rose Kennedy

October 18

There is no gloom or deep darkness where evildoers may hide themselves.

Job 34:22

Attract and Attack

Hurt people attract, then attack. As victims they somehow manage to find each other in the dark. This is surely one of the sources of discrimination. People have the ability to project their own hurt and their inferior parts on someone else whom they perceive as inferior. As they attack the weakness of the other, they feel better about themselves. Sadly, the defenses we use to hide our pain, only cause ourselves and others more pain. Through the cross, Jesus walks with us through our pain, often crying for us and blessing us at the same time.

Reflections

_____

_____

_____

_____

_____

_____

Behind every beautiful thing, there's some kind of pain.

— Bob Dylan

October 19

For he will hide me in his shelter in the day of trouble; he will conceal me under the cover of his tent; he will lift me high upon a rock.

Psalm 27:5

Defective Boundaries

Hurt people live in a realm of codependence where weak boundaries cause an ongoing problem with connectedness. With classic codependence, their hurt is hidden inside, and everybody else's problem becomes their problem. In order to avoid dealing with personal pain, the codependent focuses on someone else's problem. The problem is not with other people; the problem is with a wounded heart. Codependence can only be resolved if we are willing to confront our pain directly.

Reflections

_____

_____

_____

_____

_____

_____

Of all the animals, man is the only one that is cruel. He is the only one that inflicts pain for the pleasure of doing it.

— Mark Twain

OCTOBER 20

Answer me quickly, O Lord! My spirit fails! Hide not your face from me, lest I be like those who go down to the pit.

Psalm 143:7

THE HEART IS A SPONGE

The heart is like a sponge that becomes filled with hurt, leaving no space left for love. As a result, we cannot see beauty or experience love even if they are right in front of us. Ironically, the same people whose hearts are filled with hurt also experience a feeling of emptiness or no feeling at all. This makes relationships almost impossible.

REFLECTIONS

_____

_____

_____

_____

_____

Half the harm that is done in this world is due to people who want to feel important. They don't mean to do harm; but the harm does not interest them. Or they do not see it, or they justify it because they are absorbed in the endless struggle to think well of themselves.

— T.S. Eliot

October 21

You shall tear down their altars and break their pillars and cut down their Asherim.

Exodus 34:13

God Alternatives

There are countless alternatives to the one true God. There are addictions caused by self-absorption, which is called narcissism. There is also materialism, the desire to focus on the visible, tangible world rather than the invisible and spiritual realm. False gods can be anything including people, addictive substances, negativity, problems, or any number of unhealthy living patterns.

Reflections

_____

_____

_____

_____

_____

_____

I don't want to go on being a root in the dark,
vacillating, stretched out, shivering with sleep,
downward, in the soaked guts of the earth,
absorbing and thinking, eating each day.
— Pablo Neruda

October 22

Your altars shall become desolate, and your incense altars shall be broken, and I will cast down your slain before your idols.

Ezekiel 6:4

Godship

The issue of godship is a predominant theme in the psychology of behavior. It appears that when overwhelmed by circumstances beyond our control, human beings have a strong tendency to invest our problems with such psychological energy that they usurp the place of worship in our lives. This results in dehumanization, meaninglessness and alienation. Many of our problems do not require solutions. They need to be bowed down and surrendered to God.

Reflections

_____

_____

_____

_____

_____

_____

Godliness is more easily feigned in words than in actions.
— Jonathan Edwards, *Religious Affections*

OCTOBER 23

And we all, with unveiled face, beholding the glory of the Lord, are being transformed into the same image from one degree of glory to another.

2 Corinthians 3:18

PROJECTED IMAGES OF SELF

Recognizing that human beings have such a strong propensity to worship, we must guard against serving and ultimately being enslaved by our pseudo gods of modern culture. The end result of worshiping pseudo gods, which are no more than projected images of ourselves, is that we fuse with them and they become part of us. We must choose our gods well for we become what we worship. Similarly as we worship God and allow ourselves to be known by Him, we experience a transformation of consciousness and become the 'beloved of God'.

REFLECTIONS

_____

_____

_____

_____

_____

_____

Never forget that there are only two philosophies to rule your life: the one of the cross, which starts with the fast and ends with the feast. The other of Satan, which starts with the feast and ends with the headache.

— Fulton J. Sheen

OCTOBER 24

Where were you when I laid the foundation of the earth? Tell me, if you have understanding.

Job 38:4

KNOWING IT ALL

Since, by definition, God is all knowing and all powerful, once we have taken on godhood ourselves, we have to carry the burden of seeking to know everything and keeping total control. That means having to fight every battle, win every argument, and take charge of every situation. What an enormous and futile task! Tired and burned out, we find ourselves living defensively, wreaking havoc on our own lives, destroying our families and living below the potential that God has given us. Recognizing this, Jesus says "come unto me...and find rest for your souls". (Matthew 11:28)

REFLECTIONS

_____

_____

_____

_____

_____

_____

Every man is a divinity in disguise, a god playing the fool.
— **Ralph Waldo Emerson**

October 25

For although they knew God, they did not honor him as God or give thanks to him, but they became futile in their thinking, and their foolish hearts were darkened.

Romans 1:21

Ultimate Meaning

Human beings are religious. Frequently the search for the transcendent leads to a more purposeful life. Paul Tillich claimed that the search for ultimate meaning is the central theme of human existence. Taking it a step further, whatever we consider our ultimate concern is what we tend to worship. We are warned in the New Testament that when people have knowledge of God but refuse to cultivate worship and a life of gratitude, their thinking becomes distorted. As a result, we worship the creature rather than the creator. Gratitude is our deepest form of worship because it recognizes that all we are and have comes from God.

Reflections

Stale godliness is ungodliness. Let our religion be as warm, and constant, and natural as the flow of the blood in our veins. A living God must be served in a living way.

— Charles H. Spurgeon

October 26

Jesus said to him, "I am the way, and the truth, and the life. No one comes to the Father except through me."

John 14:6

Stinking Thinking

Alcoholics Anonymous uses the phrase *Stinking Thinking*. This distorted thinking encourages us to drown our problems with alcohol and drugs while ignoring the consequences. Such thinking is reflected in various aphorisms. For instance, "I am what I do," "I am what I feel," or "I am what I possess." Each of these represents a category of pseudo gods. We worship our jobs, we worship pleasure, and we worship material things.

Reflections

The tragedy of life is not that men do not know God. The tragedy is in knowing Him, they insist in going their own way.

— William Barclay

Good sense makes one slow to anger, and it is his glory to overlook an offense.

Proverbs 19:11

RELEVANT ANGER

It may not sound possible, but we can still have faith in God in spite of our anger, doubt and suffering. In any meaningful relationship anger is a relevant emotion and its existence indicates a connection between two people. When we become angry at someone, even though we may not know that person well, there is an automatic connection or relationship between us. Anger is a brutal gift! It is a message from our heart to come home and face ourselves. As a result, the provocation of anger may be more of a blessing than a curse.

REFLECTIONS

_____

_____

_____

_____

_____

_____

Resentment is like drinking poison and then hoping it will kill your enemies.

— Nelson Mandela

OCTOBER 28

Though he slay me, I will hope in him.

Job 13:15

WHAT COULD HAVE BEEN

In Fyodor Dostoyevsky's novel *The Idiot,* one character is dying of tuberculosis. He is angry at a universe which he believes is deaf to his excellence, his beautiful soul, and most of all to the great service he potentially might have done for mankind. On his deathbed he struggles between belief and nothingness on the one hand, and faith in the beauty and goodness of life on the other. He was living and now dying with wounded feelings. True faith is moving beyond our hurt feelings and anger to trust in God, the source and ground of our being.

REFLECTIONS

_____

_____

_____

_____

_____

_____

In many strong people there seems to be a sort of natural need--to find someone or something to bow down to.

— **Fyodor Dostoyevsky**

OCTOBER 29

For since, in the wisdom of God, the world did not know God through wisdom, it pleased God through the folly of what we preach to save those who believe.

1 Corinthians 1:21

PUTTING GOD FIRST

We do many things in life to avoid or minimize our pain. We seek experiences, objects, situations, or substances that will provide us with a sense of adequacy and well-being. The knowledge of God is both a privilege and a grave responsibility. Knowing God requires the cultivation of a spiritual relationship through prayer and worship. This is not merely religious observance, but a deep commitment to surrender our life unto the supreme authority and love of God.

REFLECTIONS

Who has seen the wind? Neither you nor I: But when the trees bow down their head, The wind is passing by.

— Christina Rossetti

October 30

Oh come, let us worship and bow down; let us kneel before the Lord, our Maker!

Psalm 95:6

Bow Down

If we refuse to bow gratefully before God, our minds lose the focus of faith. Our thoughts turn upon us, and in so doing we create pseudo gods or idols within our hearts. As religious creatures, if we refuse to bow before the one true God, we tend to create false gods and worship at their shrines in our hearts. We do well to remember that God is holy, and His glory he will not give to another.

Reflections

_____

_____

_____

_____

_____

_____

From the moment the eightenth-century French revolutionaries set up the Goddess of Reason on the high altar of Notre Dame, there wasn't a head in all Paris that was safe.

— Frederick Buechner

What profit is an idol when its maker has shaped it, a metal image, a teacher of lies? For its maker trusts in his own creation when he makes speechless idols!

Habakuk 2:18

SUPREME VALUE

It is helpful to realize that pseudo gods are created by people of faith as well as by nonbelievers. When religious persons refuse to develop true spirituality and faith, they may find themselves worshiping false gods. That passion from within, represented by the pseudo god, becomes a supreme value in a person's life. This process is not written in stone and does not always follow the same sequential order. The development of pseudo gods or idols in our lives is inevitable unless we worship the true God.

REFLECTIONS

_____

_____

_____

_____

_____

_____

Only the descent into the hell of self-knowledge can pave the way to godliness.

— Immanuel Kant

November

There is nothing that can replace the absence of someone dear to us, and one should not even attempt to do so. One must simply hold out and endure it. At first that sounds very hard, but at the same time, it is great comfort. For to the extent the emptiness remains unfilled, one remains connected to the other person through it. It is wrong to say God fills the emptiness. God in no way fills it, but much more leaves it precisely unfilled and thus helps us preserve...even in pain...the authentic relationship.

— Deitrich Bonhoeffer

NOVEMBER 1

They should seek God, and perhaps feel their way toward him and find him. Yet he is actually not far from each one of us, for "In him we live and move and have our being."

Acts 17:27-28

WOUNDS OF THE HEART

When we say that life is wounded, we do not mean that there are not many healthy areas of our life or parts of our psyche that are not wounded. Those positive aspects of our existence do not stop the negative aspects from dominating our psyches. Just as a person cannot just ignore a deep wound to the body simply because he is otherwise healthy, so it is with the wounds of the heart. They do not just get better with time. The rule of the heart is 'what you do not work out, you act out on others'. Sadly, children internalize the hurt acted out upon them, leaving them sad, confused and sometimes destroyed. Discovery means working through the hurt and shame in our heart, to release our children and those around us to experience God's beauty and grace.

REFLECTIONS

_____

_____

_____

_____

_____

_____

Stab the body and it heals, but injure the heart and the wound lasts a lifetime.

— Mineko Iwasaki

November 2

But he, knowing their thoughts, said to them, "Every kingdom divided against itself is laid to waste, and a divided household falls."

Luke 11:17

Repressing the Hurt

When we were hurt in childhood, we protected ourselves by repressing our hurt; we covered it up with a false or "coping self." The goal of the false self is to hide and protect the real self. Aware of the chronic sense of inadequacy flowing from our real, hurt self, we seek to assuage our pain and to create a greater sense of adequacy. The false self goes all out to seek anything that promises a sense of adequacy. As the split between our false and authentic selves occurs, we become a 'house divided against itself', creating a destructive tension in our lives. As a result, we are unable to experience and enjoy the wonder and beauty within and around us.

Reflections

_____

_____

_____

_____

_____

_____

He who has injured thee was either stronger or weaker than thee. If weaker, spare him; if stronger, spare thyself.

— William Shakespeare

November 3

In all circumstances take up the shield of faith, with which you can extinguish all the flaming darts of the evil one.

Ephesians 6:16

An Inadequate Defense

God, the Holy Other, is always with our hurt self. But ignoring God's presence, our false self creates pseudo gods or idols to empower us and defend against our weaknesses and inadequacies. Often, these pseudo gods seem unassailable and give us a false sense of comfort. But sadly, these false gods seduce, exploit and abandon us. When they shatter because of the piercing reality around them, we are left to fall upon our naked dependence on God's unfailing love. In essence, the pseudo god or idol promises a sense of comfort, but in the end, delivers a deeper experience of pain.

Reflections

_____

_____

_____

_____

_____

_____

A faithful friend is a strong defense; And he that hath found him hath found a treasure.

— Louisa May Alcott

You shall not make idols for yourselves or erect an image or pillar, and you shall not set up a figured stone in your land to bow down to it, for I am the Lord your God.

Leviticus 26:1

IDOL FIXATION

Our idols become our reason for being and give us meaning for living. Naturally, a greater sense of adequacy feels good so we make our pseudo gods into an end in themselves. We develop a powerful fixation. We project our inadequacies onto our idol and receive into ourselves the sense of adequacy we want to believe that it will, in turn, provide.

REFLECTIONS

I will tell you what I will do and what I will not do. I will not serve that in which I no longer believe, whether it calls itself my home, my fatherland, or my church: and I will try to express myself in some mode of life or art as freely as I can and as wholly as I can, using for my defense the only arms I allow myself to use -- silence, exile, and cunning.

— James Joyce, *A Portrait of the Artist as a Young Man*

NOVEMBER 5

He put away the male cult prostitutes out of the land and removed all the idols that his fathers had made.

1 Kings 15:12

A SENSATION OF ONENESS

Reminiscent of the early mother-child fusion, our false gods become part of us. This fusion gives us a sensation of 'oneness' and total involvement. As a result, we experience *euphoric recall*, a term used in addiction, particularly with crack addicts. It means that regardless how much suffering the drug has caused, the addict only recalls the powerful euphoria, or the high created by the drug. This illusion of selective recall interprets the past as totally positive and projects that the future will bring more of the same. There is no memory or consideration of the negative consequences and the deep hurt caused by the drug. As a result, our life becomes more fantasy than reality. Discovery on the other hand, is the unflinching commitment to face reality as it is, regardless how painful. As Merton said, 'God is the real in all that is real'.

REFLECTIONS

_____

_____

_____

_____

_____

_____

We tend to use prayer as a last resort, but God wants it to be our first line of defense. We pray when there's nothing else we can do, but God wants us to pray before we do anything at all.

— Oswald Chambers

November 6

The grass withers, the flower fades when the breath of the Lord blows on it; surely the people are grass.

Isaiah 40:7

Illusions of Permanence

Our pseudo gods become attached to our central passion, making us feel adequate and more complete. Our false god becomes our ultimate meaning, modus operandi, and hope. As a result, we seek to reconstruct reality and see our lives through the metaphoric eyes of the pseudo god. At this point we develop illusions of permanence and of omnipotence. We think that our newfound empowerment will last forever. We attribute exceptional and unlimited control to the object, our idol, leaving our lives impoverished. Sadly, a human being, who is made in the image of God, now makes the chosen object or experience into a god itself and we worship our creation rather than the creator.

Reflections

_____

_____

_____

_____

_____

_____

A long habit of not thinking a thing wrong, gives it a superficial appearance of being right, and raises at first a formidable outcry in defense of custom. But the tumult soon subsides. Time makes more converts than reason.

— **Thomas Paine**, *Common Sense*

NOVEMBER 7

You are of your father the devil, and your will is to do your father's desires. He was a murderer from the beginning, and does not stand in the truth, because there is no truth in him. When he lies, he speaks out of his own character, for he is a liar and the father of lies.

John 8:44

DENIAL AND RATIONALIZATION

Pseudo gods are seductive. We are always in danger of being seduced by the hope that our pseudo god will give us ultimate fulfillment. As a result, we subject all aspects of our lives to the idol, which leads to constriction of reality. The pseudo god reigns omnipotent in our narrow, little world. This constriction of reality involves the psychological defenses of denial and rationalization. Denial allows us to ignore or avoid particular aspects of a situation. Rationalization, on the other hand, is the choosing of an excuse to participate in a particular behavior that serves the pseudo god. These two powerful defenses block our spiritual development, leaving a void of emptiness, particularly in our prayer lives.

REFLECTIONS

_____

_____

_____

_____

_____

One is happy once one knows the necessary ingredients of happiness: simple tastes, a certain degree of courage, self denial to a point, love of work, and above all, a clear conscience.

— George Sand

NOVEMBER 8

Whatever you do, work heartily, as for the Lord and not for men.

Colossians 3:23

RECLAIMING OUR DIGNITY, MEANING, AND VALUE

God made human beings in His image. This *imago dei* means that we all have an authority card involving meaning, dignity, identity and value (M.D.I.V.). Surrender to a false god or idol is draining because we give them our authority card. Consequently our energy, ambitions and drives are dominated by our desire to please the idol. Sadly, we become easily seduced and exploited. Most seriously, when the false gods or idols shatter, we are abandoned. Painful though this may be, it is an opportunity of surrendering to God, the Eternal Love which never lets us go, and the face which never turns away.

REFLECTIONS

_____

_____

_____

_____

_____

_____

If a man is called to be a street sweeper, he should sweep streets even as a Michaelangelo painted, or Beethoven composed music or Shakespeare wrote poetry. He should sweep streets so well that all the hosts of heaven and earth will pause to say, 'Here lived a great street sweeper who did his job well'.

— Martin Luther King Jr.

Brothers, I do not consider that I have made it my own. But one thing I do: forgetting what lies behind and straining forward to what lies ahead, I press on toward the goal to win the prize for which God has called me heavenward in Christ Jesus.

Philippians 3:13-14

AN INFLATED SELF

Worshiping a false god limits our appreciation of who we are made in the image of God. This illusion leads to an inflated sense of self while at the same time diminishing the totality of our being. This exploitation and dehumanization makes us even more dependent on the false god or idol. As a result, we become what we worship; that is, we become our own god. This is dangerous because when we seek to supersede what we are, we lose who we are.

Oh God, help us to trust in thee and not in ourselves. "As for man, his days are as grass. Like the flower of the field, he flourishes. The wind passes over it and it is gone. The place thereof, knows it no more." (Psalm 103:15-16).

REFLECTIONS

_____

_____

_____

_____

_____

_____

In submission to the idol or pseudo god...they find the shadow but not the substance of the self.

— Erich Fromm

November 10

He shall seduce with flattery those who violate the covenant, but the people who know their God shall stand firm and take action.

Daniel 11:32

Seduction

As the power of the pseudo god increases, it robs us of our essential self, leading to a subtle self-destructive process. Having been seduced to see the pseudo god as ultimate fulfillment, we totally surrender ourselves. At this point, the promise of the pseudo god is thwarted, and the individual collapses under the strain. The source of the strain can come from many places such as overwork, disappointment, failure, or illness. Painful as it is, many of us refuse to know the true God until our false gods or idols shatter. Oh Lord, let our idols or false gods shatter so that we may see you more clearly...and worship you more dearly.

Reflections

When Joy [my wife] died, I had to change my idea of God to God himself, for God is the great iconoclast!

— C.S. Lewis

NOVEMBER 11

But he said to me, "My grace is sufficient for you, for my power is made perfect in weakness." Therefore I will boast all the more gladly of my weaknesses, so that the power of Christ may rest upon me.

2 Corinthians 12:9

FANTASY LAND

The false gods or idols abandon us. Abandonment is perilous, leaving us deeply hurt, angry, and wasted. The illusion of the fantasy world created by our pseudo gods is shattered by a sudden encounter with reality. We feel totally lost when alienated from our illusions. We react in anger or depression and self-destruction soon follows. The more connected we are to our pseudo gods or idols, the more vulnerable we become to the abandonment when the god is shattered by reality.

REFLECTIONS

_____

_____

_____

_____

_____

_____

I have the nerve to walk my own way, however hard, in my search for reality, rather than climb upon the rattling wagon of wishful illusions.

— Zora Neale Hurston

November 12

For now we see in a mirror dimly, but then face to face. Now I know in part; then I shall know fully, even as I have been fully known.

1 Corinthians 13:12

House of Mirrors

It is so easy to seek the visible rather than search for the invisible true God to compensate for our feelings of inadequacy. We tend to look to things, places, activities, people, and so on. Seeking to find satisfaction in these things, we give ourselves over to them, and they begin to control us. Finally, when our house of mirrors shatters, we are forced to admit and let go of the false self we thought we had become, only to be left feeling abandoned and destroyed. In this state of brokenness and despair, we often hear the soft voice of love, calling us to God and Him alone. Are you willing to quiet your heart today, so that you can hear the voice of love?

Reflections

_____

_____

_____

_____

_____

_____

Life can only be understood backwards; but it must be lived forwards.
— **Søren Kierkegaard**

NOVEMBER 13

For the Lord will have compassion on Jacob and will again choose Israel, and will set them in their own land, and sojourners will join them and will attach themselves to the house of Jacob.

Isaiah 14:1

SHATTERING ATTACHMENTS

The healing of the heart begins when God works through circumstances to shatter our pseudo gods or false images. It takes the invisible God to destroy what is destroying us. Although we identify pseudo gods as feelings, relationships, objects, appearances, money, possessions, ideologies, gambling, substances, and sex, it is an invisible, but very real, attachment to these things that God shatters. Consequently, we become open to the peace which transcends all understanding.

REFLECTIONS

_____

_____

_____

_____

_____

_____

To conceal anything from those to whom I am attached, is not in my nature. I can never close my lips where I have opened my heart.

— Charles Dickens

NOVEMBER 14

There shall not be found among you anyone who burns his son or his daughter as an offering, anyone who practices divination or tells fortunes or interprets omens, or a sorcerer.

Deuteronomy 18:10

DISILLUSIONMENT

When our false gods shatter there is much pain, disillusionment, and often despair. The void left by the loss by our pseudo god needs to be filled. This presents both a danger and an opportunity. The danger is that we have so conditioned ourselves to worship false gods to hide our real self that it is easy to return to these gods. The opportunity is to choose to worship the true God who can heal our inadequacies rather than hide them. Our choice is brief...but the consequences are endless!

REFLECTIONS

_____

_____

_____

_____

_____

_____

The point of modernity is to live a life without illusions while not becoming disillusioned.

— Antonio Gramsci

November 15

Be merciful to me, O God, be merciful to me, for in you my soul takes refuge; in the shadow of your wings I will take refuge, till the storms of destruction pass by.

Psalm 57:1

Shattered Illusions

How do we know when we are serving pseudo gods? As the power of the pseudo god increases, it robs us of our essential self. This leads to a subtle but very real self-destructiveness. Having been seduced to see the pseudo god as ultimate fulfillment, we totally surrender ourselves. At this point, any sudden confrontation with reality shatters the pseudo god whose promise is exposed as an illusion. Unfortunately, the individual collapses under the strain. At this moment, God reaches out and welcomes us in love to come to him and experience our true meaning and destiny as the beloved.

Reflections

The thinking processes attempt to organize this whole cesspool of illusions according to the laws of plausibility. This level of consciousness is supposed to reflect reality; it is the map we use for organizing our life.

— Erich Fromm

NOVEMBER 16

And behold, I am with you always, to the end of the age.

Matthew 28:20

SEVERE MERCY

Sometimes it feels like God has abandoned us, but when the chips are down he is always there with his mercy and grace. As C.S. Lewis writes, it is a severe mercy, but it is what is best for us at the time. Pseudo gods give the illusion of being there for us. As long as we live under the power of their illusion we feel safe. The only thing a pseudo god cannot tolerate is reality. That is why overwork, disappointment, failure, illness, the death of a child, or any number of personal traumas shatter the pseudo god and awaken us to the painful reality. Often this leaves us feeling empty and destroyed. As you examine your life today, is this why you feel discouraged? If this is so, remember that God's severe mercy is there for you.

REFLECTIONS

_____

_____

_____

_____

_____

_____

You have been treated with a severe mercy. You have been brought to see that you were jealous of God.

— C.S. Lewis to Sheldon Vanauaken

And he received the gold from their hand and fashioned it with a graving tool and made a golden calf. And they said, "These are your gods, O Israel, who brought you up out of the land of Egypt!"

Exodus 32:4

The Golden Calf

How often have we read the biblical story of the golden calf and thought how foolish the Israelites were to abandon the true God for a hunk of gold. They were searching for the same thing we are looking for - a god to give them a tangible connection to transcendent reality. They wanted something they could see and touch to make sense out of their journey. Once the statue was complete, the people worshiped it by dancing and singing around it. They even attributed their deliverance from slavery in Egypt to the god of the golden calf. Let us be careful in judging them because we so often forget that all we are and have comes from God. Consequently, we take things for granted, giving our allegiance to ourselves, others and things around us. As a result, we forget the true God, and create idols, which are projections of ourselves. This is no mere speculation, but a serious situation, with dire consequences for us, our family and society.

Reflections

_____

_____

_____

_____

_____

_____

Today we are less confident about our ability to find ultimate answers. We are less confident that there even are ultimate answers.

— Willard Gaylin

That which was from the beginning, which we have heard, which we have seen with our eyes, which we looked upon and have touched with our hands, concerning the word of life — this we proclaim concerning the word of life.

1 John 1:1

TOUCHED BY THE SAVIOR

God, knowing the deepest needs of his creation, satisfied our desire for a tangible connection to the transcendent by taking on flesh and blood in the incarnation of His son, the Lord Jesus Christ. Worshiping the true God, we experience a deep sense of transcendence, respect for the inestimable value of persons, and the development of community. As a result, there is a balance and harmony between inner reality (faith) and outward expression (action). This reality was reaffirmed by Mother Teresa when she encouraged us to do even 'small things with great love'!

REFLECTIONS

_____

_____

_____

_____

_____

_____

We will all see our connection with that place in each of us that honors the unquantifiable and the eternal. Our hope, our goal is that this quest for the transcendent or ultimate meaning will lead us to a more purposeful and meaningful life.

— Charles Krauthammer

Show yourself in all respects to be a model of good works, and in your teaching show integrity.

Titus 2:7

IMPOVERISHED LIFE

Pseudo gods impoverish life by destroying transcendence, meaning, dignity, and value. True community is dissolved and replaced by isolation. Certain aspects of our personhood are inflated, projected onto and passionately attached to the idol. Pseudo god worship is essentially narcissistic, limiting ourselves and others. As a result, it gives rise to the "shadow" rather than the true substance of what it means to be human. In order to clarify our faith, it may help to ask ourselves today 'are we becoming what we worship?'

REFLECTIONS

True freedom is impossible without a mind made free by discipline.
— Mortimer J. Adler

Now the Lord is the Spirit, and where the spirit of the Lord is, there is freedom.

2 Corinthians 3:17

Worship Decreases Narcissism

Faith that is based on the worship of God opens us to appreciate His goodness and mercy. The true God is the ultimate reality who shatters all idols, he is the Holy Other. Worshiping him decreases self-absorption or narcissism and enhances true personhood and community. In true worship there is harmony between the true, the good, and the beautiful. The formation of pseudo gods skews worship and seeks to make ultimate what is not ultimate. Today, let us remember that reverential fear of God is the beginning of wisdom and meaning in life.

Reflections

_____

_____

_____

_____

_____

_____

Grant me, O Lord, a mind to know you, a heart to seek you, wisdom to find you, conduct pleasing to you, faithful perseverance in waiting for you and a hope of finally embracing you.

—Thomas Aquinas

NOVEMBER 21

He who began a good work in you will carry it on to completion until the day of Jesus Christ.

Philippians 1:6

HARSH PERFECTIONISM

In true worship of God there is holiness. Holiness is not dependent upon being sinless, feeling responsible for the universe, or that you are better than everyone else. Holiness means being grasped by the goodness and grace of God. In other words, to know God is to know what it means to be forgiven. That is in contrast to a harsh perfectionism which often leads to a powerful masochistic, self-destructive process.

REFLECTIONS

_____

_____

_____

_____

_____

_____

Freeing yourself was one thing, claiming ownership of that freed self was another.

— Toni Morrison, *Beloved*

NOVEMBER 22

They promise them freedom, but they themselves are slaves of corruption. For whatever overcomes a person, to that he is enslaved.
2 Peter 2:19

FREE AND FREEING

Pseudo god formation is a hard taskmaster. Requiring total submission of the self, the pseudo god defines us and leaves no room for our true self. There is no mercy because the false god has no compassion and requires total obedience. On the other hand, worshiping God the Holy Other, the Father of our Lord Jesus Christ, is done by free will, without compulsion. Knowing God is free and freeing, a relationship that allows us to become open and loving like himself. Unfortunately, freedom comes with a price and many of us choose to enslave ourselves by worshiping false gods, rather than opening to the glorious freedom of the true God.

REFLECTIONS

_____

_____

_____

_____

_____

One word frees us of all the weight and pain of life: that word is love.
— Sophocles

A voice says, "Cry!" And I said, "What shall I cry?" All flesh is grass, and all its beauty is like the flower of the field.

Isaiah 40:6

FLOWERING OF THE HUMAN SPIRIT

Knowing God involves an integrated and balanced perspective. But when religion becomes idolatry, it becomes an end in itself. Consequently, people are used as a means to that end. Instead of true worship leading to the flowering of the human spirit, and the development of community, it seeks narcissistic gratification and control. Today let us walk in the glorious freedom of our faith in God and the love of our brothers and sisters.

REFLECTIONS

_____

_____

_____

_____

_____

We must be free not because we claim freedom, but because we practice it.

— William Faulkner

Little children, keep yourselves from idols.

1 John 5:21

God's Covenant

We are warned to avoid idol worship with its empty form and superficial knowledge of God (1 John 5:21). Idol worship is a unilateral commitment without the possibility of covenant. Human beings can be committed to anything - food, gambling, church attendance, drugs, alcohol, intellectual pursuits, academic achievement, wealth or any number of other "things." Since the gods behind our idols do not possess being or personhood, they are incapable of making a commitment in the form of a covenant to the believer for his or her worship. Covenant is only possible with another human being or with the true God, who has both being and personhood. Let us remember today that we become the product of our choices. Therefore, let us choose well. As Joshua said, "As for me and my house, we will worship the Lord" (Joshua 24:15).

Reflections

_____

_____

_____

_____

_____

_____

Covenant...includes the nine characteristics of biblical fellowship... authenticity, mercy, honesty, humility, courtesy, confidentiality, and frequency.

— Rick Warren, *The Purpose Driven Life*

November 25

Without faith, it is impossible to please God.

Hebrews 11:6

Faith

Although we have faith in God, we often refuse to bow to him. Instead we develop narcissistic tendencies to worship projected images of ourselves. It is as if we were putting God into a box saying, "If I'm going to bow to you, you have to work within this little box of mine." When the pseudo god of our self-made religion shatters, our little boxes explode, leaving us abandoned. At that point we have to bow in humility and open ourselves to the true God. Then, and only then, can we experience fellowship with God and healing for our hearts. Nevertheless, it is hard to digest the painful insight of the British poet laureate W.H. Auden, who warned that 'we would rather be ruined than changed...'

Reflections

_____

_____

_____

_____

_____

_____

Every man takes the limits of his own field of vision for the limits of the world.

— Arthur Schopenhauer

November 26

For all that is in the world — the desires of the flesh and the desires of the eyes and pride of life — is not from the Father but is from the world.

1 John 2:16

Narcissism

The most pervasive pseudo god in our modern Western culture is narcissism. Enhanced by aggressive marketing techniques and undergirded by self-focused schools of psychology, our fixation upon self is a harsh taskmaster. We struggle to achieve the right look, the best health, the proper job, the appropriate house, the perfect image...yet we always seem to fall short of our ideal.

Reflections

_____

_____

_____

_____

_____

_____

All the variety, all the charm, all the beauty of life is made up of light and shadow.

— Leo Tolstoy, *Anna Karenina*

November 27

And the haughtiness of man shall be humbled, and the lofty pride of men shall be brought low, and the Lord alone will be exalted in that day.

Isaiah 2:17

Narcissus' Self-love

According to classical Greek myth, Narcissus was a handsome young man, the heartthrob of all the nymphs who constantly threw themselves his way, yearning for his attention. He ignored all overtures and, one day, while looking into a still pool of water he saw his reflection and fell in love with his own image. Narcissus did not lack lovers, what he lacked was the ideal lover, the one that would return his gaze in perfect adoration. According to Thomas Merton, knowing God is to allow Him to become 'the transcendent source of our subjectivity'. Me plus you equals two, but me plus God is always one. Our small 'i' is swallowed up in His great 'I AM'.

Reflections

_____

_____

_____

_____

_____

_____

How many loved your moments of glad grace,
And loved your beauty with love false or true,
But one man loved the pilgrim soul in you,
And loved the sorrows of your changing face.
— W.B. Yeats

November 28

The haughty looks of man shall be brought low, and the lofty pride of men shall be humbled, and the Lord alone will be exalted in that day.

Isaiah 2:11

Rejected and Forlorn

Obsessed with his own image, Narcissus tried in vain to initiate a relationship with it. When he reached out to touch the beautiful young man in the pool, the water rippled and the image disappeared. Worse yet, at nightfall, in spite of all his begging, the image of the handsome youth refused to stay. Rejected and forlorn, Narcissus became increasingly depressed. He wasted away from his unsatisfied desire, whereupon he was transformed into the flower that bears his name.

Narcissism makes it difficult to separate what is not us from what is us. As a result, we become fused with our problems, challenges and life. Sadly, the burden becomes so heavy that we sink under load. Jesus asked his disciples to 'come apart...and rest awhile' (Mark 6:31). He calls us today to do the same, that is, to abide in his peace and love.

Reflections

_____

_____

_____

_____

_____

_____

Thoughts are the shadows of our feelings -- always darker, emptier and simpler.

— Friedrich Nietzsche

When pride comes, then comes disgrace, but with the humble is wisdom.
Proverbs 11:2

NARCISSISTIC PERSONALITY

In psychiatry, a narcissistic personality is a personality disorder characterized by extreme self-centeredness and self-absorption, fantasies involving unrealistic goals, an excessive need for attention and admiration, and disturbed interpersonal relationships. In psychoanalytic terms, narcissism is an erotic gratification derived from admiration of one's own physical or mental attributes. A normal condition at the infantile level of personality development, narcissism in later stages is an inordinate preoccupation with the self. Therefore, it is nearly impossible to reach out to others. Knowing God is self-actualization, where we reach beyond ourselves to touch the souls of others.

REFLECTIONS

_____

_____

_____

_____

_____

_____

so I love you because I know no other way than this:
where I does not exist, nor you,
so close that your hand on my chest is my hand,
so close that your eyes close as I fall asleep.
— Pablo Neruda

One's pride will bring him low, but he who is lowly in spirit will obtain honor.

Proverbs 29:23

SHRINE OF NARCISSISM

Today's world breeds narcissism. Modern pressures in the home and family rob children of adequate nurturing experiences, creating narcissistic tendencies. When combined with our society's diminishing appreciation of transcendence and worship, this pattern pushes countless men and women to sacrifice themselves at the shrine of narcissism.

REFLECTIONS

_____

_____

_____

_____

_____

_____

For like a shaft, clear and cold, the thought pierced him that in the end the Shadow was only a small and passing thing: there was light and high beauty for ever beyond its reach.

— J.R.R. Tolkien, *The Return of the King*

December

We shall not cease from exploration and the end of our exploring will be to arrive where we started and know the place for the first time.

— T. S. Eliot

DECEMBER 1

This is my comfort in my affliction, that your promise gives me life.
Psalm 119:50

STABILITY, CONSISTENCY, AND PREDICTABILITY

The development of a healthy sense of self requires stability, consistency, and predictability in the child's environment. All too often in a dysfunctional family, however, these qualities are absent, and the child does not properly internalize the mother. Instead, an inner void is created in the child as manifested by severe love hunger, poor self-esteem, poor frustration tolerance, and inadequate identity formation.

Similarly, spirituality requires stability, consistency and predictability for us to grow in God. As we surrender to God, the unchanging core in a changing world, we come to abide in Him, and He in us. How incomprehensible that our bodies are the temple of the living God! Living in contemplation with this awareness opens us to the mystery and beauty of life. This is discovery!

REFLECTIONS

_____

_____

_____

_____

_____

_____

Our vocation is not simply to be, but to work together with God in the creation of our own life, our own identity, our own destiny.
— Thomas Merton

DECEMBER 2

But whoever causes one of these little ones who believe in me to sin, it would be better for him to have a great millstone fastened around his neck and to be drowned in the depth of the sea.

Matthew 18:6

VULNERABLE CHILDREN

Everyone knows that children in the process of development are vulnerable to the stresses and strains of their environment. When a child is hurt by loss, rejection, or abuse (physical, sexual, or emotional), the child withdraws into himself. Unable to cope with the pain, a child represses the real hurt and develops a false self.

It is important to note that children are also traumatized by over-indulgence. Giving too much to a child develops a sense of narcissistic entitlement. The child begins to believe that life owes him everything. In reality this is not true, so in time the child becomes hurt, disappointed, and his sense of entitlement is transformed to narcissistic rage, despair and depression.

REFLECTIONS

_____

_____

_____

_____

_____

_____

We owe our children – the most vulnerable citizens in any society – a life free from violence and fear.

— Nelson Mandela

December 3

For whoever would save his life will lose it, but whoever loses his life for my sake will save it. For what does it profit a man if he gains the whole world and loses or forfeits himself?

Luke 9:24-25

Me, Me, Me

Narcissism in today's world is reflected in the regression to childish modes of thinking and characteristic behavior. Simply put, we seek self-absorption, self-gratification and control, manifested by such thoughts as:

"Take care of number one."
"All for me."
"I'm sorry it happened to you, but I'm glad it's not me."
"Do your own thing."
"I did it my way."

After our Lord's baptism, he taught 'repent, for the kingdom of God is at hand...it is within you'. Repentance means turning from our way and surrendering to God's love. To do this, our selfish self must die as we open to our true self as the 'beloved of God'.

Reflections

_____

_____

_____

_____

_____

_____

Every man must decide whether he will walk in the light of creative altruism or in the darkness of destructive selfishness.

— Martin Luther King Jr.

December 4

A new commandment I give to you, that you love one another: just as I have loved you, you also are to love one another.

John 13:34

Prosperity religion

Creeping into the churches, modern narcissistic philosophy preaches a prosperity gospel: serve God and you will be rich, healthy, and prosperous. How starkly this contrasts with Christ who had to experience the cross, the crucible of suffering, even though he served God faithfully. While on earth, Christ lived between the transfiguration pole (i.e. glory) and the Gethsemane pole (i.e. suffering). The Christian life is always lived between these two poles.

Similarly, psychology, although promising to help a person self-actualize, may condone a total focus on the self. This will cause the individual to become more selfish, self-centered, and unable to empathize with others. True self-actualization should always lead us beyond ourselves.

Reflections

_____

_____

_____

_____

_____

_____

Selfishness is not living as one wishes to live, it is asking others to live as one wishes to live.

— Oscar Wilde

December 5

I have said these things to you, that in me you may have peace. In the world you will have tribulation. But take heart! I have overcome the world.

John 16:33

Family Discord

Perhaps nowhere else has the prevailing narcissistic philosophy been more destructive than in the family. As mothers and fathers worship at the throne of narcissism, the sense of sacrifice, intimate sharing, and community bonding is a fast disappearing phenomenon. As parents preach and act out, "I want it my own way," children follow suit and live accordingly. The end result is dehumanization and discord.

The coming of Christ overcomes our shame and destroys our fear of death, giving us the courage to live in love, compassion and hope.

Reflections

_____

_____

_____

_____

_____

_____

What can you do to promote world peace? Go home and love your family.

— Mother Teresa

December 6

May the God of hope fill you with all joy and peace in believing, so that by the power of the Holy Spirit you may abound in hope.

Romans 15:13

A Transcendental Vacuum

Being created in the image of God, the *imago dei*, means that human beings have a God-space, or what I term a transcendental vacuum, which can only be filled by God himself. The narcissistic craving propels human beings to seek fulfillment through false gods. Although we are made in the image of God, we are flawed and the concept of being flawed runs counter to our desired, positive self-image. The dichotomy between good self-image and flawed human nature has made us cynical and has produced a crisis of faith in our belief in human nature. Recognizing our plight, God sent His son to shine upon us who sit in darkness (shame) and the shadow of death to lead us into the way of peace (Luke 1: 78-79).

Reflections

_____

_____

_____

_____

_____

_____

True wisdom consists of two things: (a) knowledge of God and (b) knowledge of the self.

— **John Calvin**

DECEMBER 7

Do not be conformed to this world, but be transformed by the renewal of your mind, that by testing you may discern what is the will of God, what is good and acceptable and perfect.

Romans 12:2

MINDLESS CONFORMITY

Conformity is a powerful dynamic in our culture. The pressure to conform causes us to live in fear of creativity. We blend into the crowd in order to hide our uniqueness, our individuality. The urge to fit in, to keep up with the neighbors, and to please each other creates mindless conformity. That kind of behavior is devoid of creativity. Fearing our own individuality and nursing our fragile identities, we spend our years lusting after the attributes of others. In the process, we end up hopelessly mediocre. Sir John Templeton reminds us 'change your mind...change your world'.

REFLECTIONS

_____

_____

_____

_____

_____

_____

To be yourself in a world that is constantly trying to make you something else is the greatest accomplishment.

— Ralph Waldo Emerson

But we have this treasure in jars of clay, to show that the surpassing power belongs to God and not to us.

2 Corinthians 4:7

IDENTITY CONFUSION

On the one hand, conformity creates a dynamic in which we refuse to use our talents, vision, and creativity because we fear criticism, failure, or rejection. Bowing down to the god of conformity is due to our lack of acceptance or appreciation of our own identity. This creates a frantic effort to please and follow others to establish our authority card, which is comprised of our meaning, dignity, identity and value. As a result, we become externally controlled rather than internally directed.

REFLECTIONS

_____

_____

_____

_____

_____

_____

Most people are other people. Their thoughts are someone else's opinions, their lives a mimicry, their passions a quotation.

— Oscar Wilde

We are his workmanship created in Christ unto good works ordained for us before the foundation of the world.

Ephesians 2: 10

THE CALL TO SERVE

God has called us to participate courageously in his divinity by being his instruments of creativity in the world. Sadly, our desire to fit in or conform blocks the divine will for our lives. Blending in with the crowd, we lose our uniqueness, leaving us bored and lonely. Unable to be nurtured in our inner life by God's love, we choose to drink from our own cisterns even though they are inadequate, and cannot satisfy us. God says to Jeremiah 'For My people have committed two evils: They have forsaken Me, the fountain of living waters, and hewn them out cisterns – broken cisterns that can hold no water" (Jeremiah 2:13). Our challenge today, as we rush around doing our daily chores, is not to forget our most precious treasure – Christ in us, the hope of glory.

REFLECTIONS

_____

_____

_____

_____

_____

_____

The awful importance of this life is that it determines eternity.
— William Barclay

December 10

And in the last days it shall be, God declares, that I will pour out my Spirit on all flesh, and your sons and your daughters shall prophesy, and your young men shall see visions, and your old men shall dream dreams.

Acts 2:17

Identity Crisis

Teenagers are particularly susceptible to conformity. Ages 11 to 21 are the years of identity formation. Conformity is a borrowed identity. It often takes the form of the current anti-establishment craze among young people, often found in that generation's music. In the roaring 20's it was the Charleston and fringe dresses, the 30's saw the zoot-suiters, the 40's the big bands and swing dancing, the 50's was Elvis and beatniks, the 60's was rock 'n roll, and so on. As teenagers, we were trying to find ourselves, but in reality, we were hiding from our true selves by conforming to the crowd. The loneliness of the crowd is one major factor in the high rate of suicides among teens.

Sadly the teenage phenomenon of identity diffusion and crises continues into adulthood. Our God sent his son Christ into our world, to encourage us to mature and live in love. 'Joy to the world, the Lord has come'. Christ came into the world to liberate us from our identity confusion so that we can experience the deeper meaning of life as the 'beloved of God'.

Reflections

_____

_____

_____

Our youth now love luxury. They have bad manners, contempt for authority; they show disrespect for their elders and love chatter in place of exercise; they no longer rise when elders enter the room; they contradict their parents, chatter before company; gobble up their food and tyrannize their teachers.

— Socrates

December 11

For unto us a child is born, to us a son is given, and the government will be upon his shoulder.

Isaiah 9:6

MATURITY

Life is wounded and we face many different challenges. Strange as it may seem, we can only mature if we're willing to face our suffering, set-backs and disappointments. So often, we have a childish illusion that life is fair, only to suddenly awake to the reality that bad things happen even to 'good people'. As we approach the Christmas season, it is important for us to recognize that God identifies with our plight. He came to us in the baby Jesus, born in poverty, outside the mainstream of society. Sadly, this event has become so familiar to us that it has lost its mystery and potent effect on our lives. As we ponder the reality that God in Christ came into our world to identify with our suffering and challenges in life, we rediscover the meaning of Christmas.

REFLECTIONS

_____

_____

_____

_____

_____

_____

Every happening, great and small, is a parable whereby God speaks to us, and the art of life is to get the message.

— Malcom Muggeridge

December 12

As obedient children, do not be conformed to the passions of your former ignorance.

1 Peter 1:14

Pathway to Conformity

Codependency is another pathway to conformity. Codependent individuals are wounded in life due to painful family dynamics, physical, emotional, or sexual abuse, or other traumas. The hurt, which can occur in childhood or any other time in life, interrupts the development of a meaningful identity, and the individuals become dependent on other persons to meet their needs. The result is a poor development of self and the creation of distorted and painful relationships.

God challenges us to be transformed by the renewing of our minds (Romans 12:1). For instance, at Christmas, the shepherds - a group of disenfranchised, poor persons - were surprised by joy, when the angels sang 'glory to God in the highest, and on earth, peace and goodwill to all persons' (Luke 2:14). Similarly, if we're willing to face our pain, the Christ child comes to lead us into the way of healing and peace.

Reflections

_____

_____

_____

_____

_____

_____

To be one's self, and unafraid whether right or wrong, is more admirable than the easy cowardice of surrender to conformity.

— Irving Wallace

Beloved, do not imitate evil but imitate good. Whoever does good is from God; whoever does evil has not seen God.

3 John 1:11

VULNERABILITY AND INADEQUACY

Conformity is powerful, giving us the desire to please, be perfect, and have total control. Facing our vulnerability and inadequacy, we are unable to stand on our own, and find ourselves willing to give up anything to please or be part of the group. There is nothing wrong in trying to please or cooperate with one's group. But when fitting in becomes an end in itself so that the individual has no sense of identity, self-destruction occurs. Sadly, as we face our shattered dreams and the brokenness of our life, it is so easy to become confused and live in despair. Nevertheless in the darkness of our despair, we hear afresh the bells of Christmas, reminding us that God has joined us on our journey of pain and suffering.

REFLECTIONS

Clasping the hands in prayer is the beginning of the uprising against the disorder of the world.

— Karl Barth

DECEMBER 14

Complete my joy by being of the same mind, having the same love, being in full accord and of one mind.

Philippians 2:2

THE SEPARATION PROCESS

As with narcissism, the dynamic of conformity occurs early in our development. We were a "we" (fusion with mother) initially, before we became an "I" (differentiation). Moreover, we have to become an "I" again (sense of identity) before we can become a "we" (in relationship to others). Life develops as a separation individuation process. But life is wounded and batters us in so many ways. Christmas reminds us that the baby Jesus is born afresh in our hearts.

Prayer: Lord, knowing you is all about you, and not about me. I don't have the depth of consciousness to really know you. So I rest in knowing that my love for you is you actually loving me. Thus to know you is to be known by you. Amen.

REFLECTIONS

_____

_____

_____

_____

_____

_____

God loves each of us as if there were only one of us.

— St. Augustine

December 15

Glory to God in the highest, and on earth, peace to men on whom his favor rests.

Luke 2:14

From Fear to Love

The annunciation of the birth of Christ is a perceptual shift from fear to love. All feelings can be reduced to fear and shame or love and compassion. The message of Christmas is to let go of fear and shame and open up to love and compassion. The angels' words have offered hope and encouragement for shame-based human beings throughout the years.

Reflections

_____

_____

_____

_____

_____

_____

This set down
    This: were we led all that way for
    Birth or Death? There was a Birth, certainly,
    We had evidence and no doubt. I had seen birth and death,
    But had thought they were different; this Birth was
    Hard and bitter agony for us, like Death, our death.
    We returned to our places, these kingdoms,
    But no longer at ease here, in the old dispensation,
    With an alien people clutching their gods.
    I should be glad of another death.
                — **T.S. Eliot**, "The Journey of the Magi"

DECEMBER 16

But when you give to the needy, do not let your left hand know what your right hand is doing.

Matthew 6:3

ALTRUISM OR CODEPENDENCE

Sometimes codependents seem to be good people acting out of altruistic motives. They would deny that they are people pleasers. They genuinely want to do good things for others. But without proper boundaries, individuals lose their sense of being who they really are. By contrast, when we give altruistically, we do so from the center of our identity, which is intact. In other words, we are not giving to get an identity or to impress or to be loved. We are simply sharing out of the identity of our own personhood.

REFLECTIONS

_____

_____

_____

_____

_____

_____

You have not lived today until you have done something for someone who can never repay you.

— John Bunyan

DECEMBER 17

Or who shut in the sea with doors
when it burst out from the womb,
when I made clouds its garment
and thick darkness its swaddling band,
and prescribed limits for it
and set bars and doors,
and said, 'Thus far shall you come, and no farther,
and here shall your proud waves be stayed'?

Job 38:8-11

BOUNDARIES

The contra-dependent, like the codependent, is a deeply hurt individual carrying a burden of anger, fear, shame, and guilt. But contra-dependents have a problem making connections with people. Because of the hurt inside them, they have rigid boundaries instead of porous ones like the codependent. They have built fortresses around themselves. The idea is to be so well insulated that no further injury can occur. Christmas means that God sent His son to be with us. In fact, the meaning of Christmas is God with us. This reality allows us to face our pain and open ourselves, in love, to God and to each other.

REFLECTIONS

_____

_____

_____

_____

_____

_____

His weakness was his belief that evil had boundaries.
— Erik Larson

December 18

We always thank God, the Father of our Lord Jesus Christ, when we pray for you, because we have heard of your faith in Christ Jesus and of the love you have for all God's people – the faith and love that spring from the hope stored up for you in heaven and about which you have already heard in the true message of the gospel.

Colossians 1:3-5

The Need for Hope

Not surprisingly, contra-dependents attract codependents. A codependent and contra-dependent make a very interesting couple. Contra-dependents feel empty and need someone to bring them hope; the codependent has weak boundaries and wants to love or to please. Between these two wounded individuals, natural coalescence occurs. However, problems arise when a contra-dependent goes into therapy and weakens his boundaries, producing the potential for two codependents.

Similarly, codependents, in therapy, strengthen their boundaries, and move toward becoming contra-dependent. It is important for both individuals to recognize their need for growth and to somehow work together, realizing that when one goes into therapy, the other will be profoundly affected. These relationships are painful and challenging. But God is the God of all comfort and love, and is able to provide a balm of healing and peace. At this Christmastime, the real message is that what looks like a catastrophe explodes into joy. "Joy to the world, the Lord has come."

Reflections

_____

_____

_____

_____

Darkness cannot drive out darkness: only light can do that. Hate cannot drive out hate: only love can do that.

— Martin Luther King, Jr.

December 19

You shall stand up before the gray head and honor the face of an old man, and you shall fear your God: I am the Lord.

Leviticus 19:32

Dignity Theft

The pseudo god of conformity may be manifested in persons who give totally of themselves in order to please, in the hope that they will receive love. It may also be manifested in the contra-dependent who feels utterly empty inside, and therefore chooses to control others. The two may become fused and interdependent with each other. Pseudo god formation occurs when these particular issues became an end in themselves, robbing individuals of their inherent dignity and rights. When the resultant codependency or contra-dependency becomes the driving force in life, it becomes a false god.

Reflections

_____

_____

_____

_____

_____

I can say that I never knew what joy was like until I gave up pursuing happiness, or cared to live until I chose to die. For these two discoveries I am beholden to Jesus.

— Malcolm Muggeridge

December 20

For this reason I bow my knees before the Father, from whom every family in heaven and on earth is named.

Ephesians 3:14-15

Family

Family life can be a blessing or very painful. Sometimes our kids do not perform brilliantly or even acceptably. Sometimes financial crisis occurs, robbing us of our house, possessions, and the easygoing lifestyle that made family life so contented. Sometimes sickness or death intrudes, leaving us vulnerable and confused. Crises leave the idolized family reeling, because until that point the family unit has operated under the illusion of invulnerability. As Christmas approaches, it is important to recognize that we need to make space for God. Mary made space for God, and the baby Jesus came. At the inn, there was no space, and the baby Jesus passed by. The shepherds made space for God, and found the baby Jesus in the manger. Similarly, at this very busy and joyous time of the year, it is so easy for us to forget to make space for God. Even though we go through the motions of celebrating Christmas, we once again miss the vision and lose the reality of the meaning of 'peace on earth, and goodwill to all persons'. Let us determine to make a difference this Christmas.

Reflections

_____

_____

_____

_____

All parents damage their children. It cannot be helped. Youth, like pristine glass, absorbs the prints of its handlers. Some parents smudge, others crack, a few shatter childhoods completely into jagged little pieces, beyond repair.

— Mitch Albom

DECEMBER 21

Fathers, do not provoke your children to anger, but bring them up in the discipline and instruction of the Lord.

Ephesians 6:4

DESTRUCTIVE EXPECTATIONS

We also see family idolatry when parents actually fuse with their children. When that happens, the child's performances at school, in sports activities, or in musical performances, affect the parents' self-esteem. One only has to watch parents at a little league game to see this tendency in action. When our kids become an obsession, we become fused to them. As a result, when they do poorly we become anxious and upset, but when they do well we feel better. There can be a powerful connection between the progress or the performance of the child and the emotional state of the parent. It is difficult to achieve the balance between our expectations and the actual accomplishment of our children. This causes much pain and conflict. It is so important to surrender our children to God in prayer each day, asking his blessings and guidance in their lives.

REFLECTIONS

_____

_____

_____

_____

_____

_____

Parents can only give good advice or put them on the right paths, but the final forming of a person's character lies in their own hands.

— Anne Frank

December 22

For they loved the glory that comes from man more than the glory that comes from God.

John 12:43

Public Impressions

Within some families there is a conformity issue related to being part of the "right kind of family." Those people in the popular crowd feel superior to those who are "out." This dysfunction extends beyond families into clubs, organizations, school loyalty, patriotism, ethnic nationality, racism, and political affiliation. This dynamic results in prejudices and even cruelty to others outside the group because we are unable to accept the views of others that differ from our own. Christmas is inclusive. Christ came to bring peace and hope to all families – i.e. the world. He is not only the gentle Jesus, meek and mild. He is the cosmic Christ.

Reflections

_____

_____

_____

_____

_____

_____

Fame is a vapor, popularity is an accident, riches take wings, those who cheer today may curse tomorrow and only one thing endures - character.
— Harry S. Truman

Therefore, if anyone is in Christ, he is a new creation. The old has passed away; behold, the new has come.

2 Corinthians 5:17

CULTURAL CONFORMITY

The pseudo god of conformity also manifests itself in the fads that emerge within our culture, particularly in areas such as fashion apparel, interior decoration, status cars, or trends in sports activities. Many of us try to fit in willy-nilly without thinking through our choices. We may be driving to "keep up with the Joneses" and finding ourselves living beyond our means. Sometimes, because we cannot afford to compete, we punish ourselves with the idea that we would only be happy if we could live in the right house, on the right street, in the right part of town, or provide for our children a better life than we had. But as Christmas approaches, let us stop and meditate on the fact that our longing for acceptance and fulfillment is a longing for God himself. As Saint Augustine said, "We shall ever restless be, until we find our rest in thee".

REFLECTIONS

_____

_____

_____

_____

_____

_____

Your time is limited, so don't waste it living someone else's life. Don't be trapped by dogma - which is living with the results of other people's thinking. Don't let the noise of other's opinions drown out your own inner voice.

— Steve Jobs

December 24

We should not be like Cain, who was of the evil one and murdered his brother. And why did he murder him? Because his own deeds were evil and his brother's righteous.

1 John 3:12

Controlling Others

Sometimes inner hurt drives people to control others. We see this demonstrated in the demagogic control such people as David Koresh and Jim Jones held over their followers. I suspect that the cult leader has a tremendous sense of inadequacy. They have the ability to split off the disavowed inadequate parts and project them onto people who are hurt. The followers are willing to internalize the leader's inadequate parts, and bow in submission to them.

The fact is we are all inadequate and flawed. Recognizing the plight of our dilemma, Christmas means that God reaches out to us to share our life and experience. Christmas is universal, but most of all, it is personal. Christ came into the world, but more importantly, he came into our lives. Let us bow down and worship, for God is with us.

Reflections

_____

_____

_____

_____

_____

_____

Unless we have the courage to fight for a revival of wholesome reserve between man and man, we shall perish in an anarchy of human values... . Socially it means the renunciation of all place-hunting, a break with the cult of the "star".

— Dietrich Bonhoeffer

DECEMBER 25

For unto you is born this day, in the city of David, a savior, which is Christ the Lord.

Luke 2:11

CHRISTMAS

It is Christmas. Today we celebrate the birth of our Lord. Let us open to the peace and joy of this special occasion. This means we have to stop, look and listen. This is not easy because we are pulled by our busyness, excitement, frivolity and the goodwill of the season. Let us determine to keep the awareness of our visitation. Let the Christ child be born in us afresh today. This is no mere sentimentality, but is expressed in our choosing to live in love with ourselves and each other.

REFLECTIONS

_____

_____

_____

_____

_____

Magna est veritas et semper prae valebit.
Great is the truth, and it will always prevail.
— Unknown

DECEMBER 26

For those whom he foreknew he also predestined to be conformed to the image of his Son, in order that he might be the firstborn among many brothers.

Romans 8:29

CHRISTMAS PAST

As the climax of Christmas fades, we find ourselves being tired, talked out, sad, and often frustrated. In the post-holiday blues, we have to stop and rest, to allow God's love to caress and permeate us. This means desiring to live in the house of love to gaze upon the beauty of God and to worship Him in His temple. Only then can we be renewed and refreshed to continue the mission of God's love in the world.

REFLECTIONS

_____

_____

_____

_____

_____

_____

I will honor Christmas in my heart, and try to keep it all the year.
— Charles Dickens

DECEMBER 27

For I am not ashamed of the gospel...for in it the righteousness of God is revealed from faith for faith, as it is written, "The righteous shall live by faith."

Romans 1:16-17

THE GOSPEL

The gospel is the good news. It is God's story which becomes interwoven into our story. Christ has come. Fear and death are destroyed and LOVE wins. Of course, this is easier said than experienced. But today, let it sink into our hearts that God loves us as we are. With our failures, sins, shortcomings and mess-ups, His unfailing love caresses us and holds us to himself. The experience of being loved by God, the ultimate mystery, casts out all doubt and fear...and opens us to forgiveness, gratitude and peace.

REFLECTIONS

_____

_____

_____

_____

_____

_____

Faith sees the invisible, believes the unbelievable, and receives the impossible.

— Corrie Ten Boom

DECEMBER 28

And Jesus answered him, "It is written, 'Man shall not live by bread alone.'"

Luke 4:4

STONES INTO BREAD

Materialism is so powerful that Satan used it to tempt the Son of God in the wilderness. Jesus was physically weak and vulnerable after forty days of fasting. The evil one challenged him to prove his divinity by turning stones into bread.

The challenge to turn stones into bread is always with us. We are especially vulnerable when weakened by hunger, poverty, or financial collapse. But in spite of our situation, we do well to heed the words of Jesus that we 'cannot live by bread alone, but by every word that proceeds from God'. Jesus said his words are life and spirit (John 6:63). Therefore when his words are internalized, they produce the fruit of the spirit: love, peace and joy. Even though we may have all our material needs met, what is life without love, peace and joy?

REFLECTIONS

First, we break bread and drink wine together, telling the story of Jesus and his death, because Jesus knew that this set of actions would explain the meaning of his death in a way that nothing else--no theories, no clever ideas — could ever do.

— N.T. Wright

DECEMBER 29

He himself bore our sins in his body on the tree, that we might die to sin and live to righteousness. By his wounds you have been healed.

1 Peter 2:24

CHARACTER SCARS

Suffering is best endured when seen through the cross where Christ suffered and died. He still carries the scars from those wounds. It was by the wounds of his suffering that Christ revealed himself to Thomas who doubted the resurrection. Upon being shown the wounds of Christ, he uttered the only response possible, "My Lord and my God." As we suffer, we identify with our Lord, the One who suffered for us. When we see our own suffering through the wounded body of Christ, we learn the deeper meaning of life, one that we could never know if we did not experience suffering. Suffering is a painful, but thorough teacher. Life is about learning. Until we learn the lessons, we often have to repeat them. This occurs in the crucible of suffering, sometimes leaving us with many scars. But the power of the gospel is that it turns our 'scars into stars' and 'wounds into wisdom'.

REFLECTIONS

_____

_____

_____

_____

_____

_____

God will not look you over for medals, degrees or diplomas but for scars.
— Elbert Hubbard

DECEMBER 30

Although he was a son, he learned obedience through what he suffered.

Hebrews 5:8

THE WOUNDED GOD

Jesus is the wounded God. He has participated in our suffering and knows the hurt trail of our lives because he has walked it himself. The difference between our suffering and his is that we have brought a lot of our suffering upon ourselves through our own failures. The good news is that forgiveness is available when we invite Christ to walk along side us on the path of the wounded life. Forgiveness releases hurt feelings and, if necessary, brings them from the unconscious to the conscious. Once they are conscious, we are able to disconnect the hurtful experience from the painful feelings. In other words, a hurt feeling is connected to a particular experience that gives it a negative energy in our lives. While these experiences are not forgotten, forgiveness shuts off their power and heals the hurt in our hearts.

REFLECTIONS

_____

_____

_____

_____

_____

_____

Character cannot be developed in ease and quiet. Only through experience of trial and suffering can the soul be strengthened, vision cleared, ambition inspired, and success achieved.

— Helen Keller

If I am guilty, woe to me! If I am in the right, I cannot lift up my head, for I am filled with disgrace and look on my affliction.

Job 10:15

THE CROSS OF CHRIST

Shame and guilt stalk us all our lives. Shame is how we view ourselves, and guilt relates to our behavior. For example, shame is 'I am a mistake' while guilt is 'I made a mistake'. Because of the power of these two major issues in our lives, we need to be constantly open to God's forgiveness. Shame and guilt are so pervasive, we spend much of our lives seeking to compensate or atone for them. This may take the form of self-destructive punishing acts or different types of penance. There is always going to be a gap between our ideals (love of God and love of neighbor) and our behavior. Shame and guilt separate us from God, but forgiveness comes through union with him through the cross of Jesus Christ. Whenever we fail to live up to God's standard of love, let the cross of Christ occupy that gap and shame and guilt will flee away. Remember, the cross of Christ is not only for our eternal salvation, but it's also the power of God which allows us to conquer the prevailing effects of shame and guilt in our daily experience.

REFLECTIONS

_____

_____

_____

_____

Every one of us is shadowed by an illusory person: a false self. We're not very good at identifying illusions, least of all, the ones we cherish about ourselves. Contemplation is not and cannot be a function of this external self...we can rise above this unreality and recover our hidden reality. God himself begins to live in [us], not only as creator, but as [our] other and true self.

— Thomas Merton, *New Seeds of Contemplation*